WE ARE OUR MOTHERS' DAUGHTERS

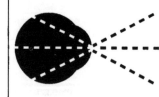

This Large Print Book carries the
Seal of Approval of N.A.V.H.

WE ARE OUR MOTHERS' DAUGHTERS

Cokie Roberts

Thorndike Press • Thorndike, Maine

Published in 1998 by arrangement with
William Morrow & Co., Inc.

Thorndike Large Print® Americana Series.

The tree indicium is a trademark of Thorndike Press.

The text of this Large Print edition is unabridged.
Other aspects of the book may vary from the original edition.

Set in 16 pt. Plantin by Al Chase.

Printed in the United States on permanent paper.

Library of Congress Cataloging in Publication Data
Roberts, Cokie.
    We are our mothers' daughters / Cokie Roberts. — Large
print ed.
      p.   cm.
   ISBN 0-7862-1626-3 (lg. print : hc : alk. paper)
    1. Women — United States — History. 2. Sex
discrimination against women — United States.
3. Feminism — United States. 4. Roberts, Cokie.
5. Women journalists — United States — Biography.
I. Title.
[HQ1421.R63 1998b]
  305.42′0973—dc21   98-28012

This book is about women. But it would not be possible without a man. To my husband, Steven — my mentor, my fan, my lover, my muse — this book is dedicated.

Contents

Acknowledgments

Any time I undertake a project of any size, it means my friends and family have undertaken it as well. This one was no exception, so there are many to thank. First thanks to the folks at Morrow: Bill Wright and Paul Fedorko, who decided this book was a good idea; my friend and editor, Claire Wachtel, who pushed me to do it; and Sharyn Rosenblum and Karen Auerbach, who made it possible for people to know it exists. They've been helped in that effort by Su Lin Cheng at ABC News. Also at ABC, Robin Sproul has been the most supportive of bosses and my good friends and colleagues Sam Donaldson, Dorrance Smith, and Virginia Moseley have had to put up with my distraction while getting this done. So has my friend and producer Ellen McDonnell at NPR. My dear friend Ann Charnley has been my buddy for more than thirty years. I knew she was just the right person to ask for help in researching these themes, and, in the way of women, she knew that Alice Shrock, professor of history at Earlham College, was just the right person to guide her. Lauren Burke, my assistant for several years, aided with the research as well. Along with Anne McGinn, she also helped me deal with the manuscript — from taming the computer, to faxing and FedExing. Kim Roellig kept the rest of my life going so that not too much fell through the cracks. Bob Barnett is more than a lawyer, he's a friend, and he never points me in the wrong direction. And to my mother, mother-in-law, daughter, daughter-in-law, sister, sisters-in-law, great-grandmothers, grandmothers, great-aunts, aunts, tantes, teachers, nieces, great-nieces, cousins, and friends, plus American women past and present — thank you for providing the material.

Introduction:
We Are Our Mothers' Daughters

What is woman's place? That's been the hot question of my adult life. From the boardrooms to the bedrooms of the country's companies and couples the debate over the role of women has created enormous upheaval for society and for the family. For women like me, who grew up and graduated from college before the revolution, it's all gotten a little exhausting. We were the vanguard, not necessarily in philosophical terms but in practical ones. Most of us weren't engaged in fighting for the feminist cause, but we were busy — unbelievably busy — living it, either consciously or unconsciously. We went with our shiny degrees pouring into the work force as the first generation of women with the law on our side. When I graduated from Wellesley in 1964 it was perfectly legal to discriminate against women in the workplace. When we applied for jobs, the men we were applying to regularly and with no embarrassment told us, "We don't hire women to do that." But the 1964 Civil Rights Act was passed that summer and, though it took a while for any of us to realize it, the workplace terrain underwent a seismic shift. (The men who wrote the Civil Rights Act had no intention of changing the lives of women, and therefore men, so dramatically, but that's a tale for another place in these pages.)

We were the pioneers — or so we thought. And in many ways we were. We were the first women at almost everything we did, and most of us often had the experience of being the only woman in the room. Unlike the few women who preceded us in the world of work, who in most cases were singular obstacle-leaping females, we arrived as an entire generation of educated and, in our minds at least, equal-to-men women. We have the scars to show that we knocked down barriers rather than jump over them, making it easier for the women who followed us. (We've been known to grow a little grumpy over the ingratitude of young women, for their sometimes smug assumption that all that "woman stuff" is passé, ancient history. We find ourselves muttering, like the Wicked Witch of the West, "Just you wait, my pretty.")

The brave new world we were forging took its toll — many of our youthful, pre-liberation marriages didn't survive. The rules changed so fundamentally from the ones in place on our wedding days that it took more than the usual amount of adaptation to make those unions work. I'm one of the lucky ones. At the age of eighteen I spotted the perfect husband, and finally convinced him to propose when I was an almost-over-the-hill twenty-two. With good senses of humor, and incredible generosity on his part, Steven and I have happily managed for more than thirty years to make it over the shoals of constantly shifting expectations.

Now here's our generation, women in our fifties, with grown daughters taking on the challenges of work and family. There's a lot of reassessment going on, and a lot of re-writing of history. There's also a lot of foolish rehashing of old debates as privileged women who have the choice of whether to earn a paycheck engage in finger pointing at women who make different choices than they do. I must admit this often vituperative argument about staying home versus going to work makes me nuts. It's not men who are doing this to women, it's women who are doing it to each other, trying to validate the decisions they make by denigrating the decisions of others.

Over the decades, as I witnessed and participated in this great social movement of the century, I had only one real fear for women: that we would lose our sense of perspective. Our great strength, in my view, has been our ability to see beyond the concerns of the day. As the nurturers, the caregivers, we have always worried about the future — what it will mean for the children — and as the custodians and carriers of the culture, we've carefully kept alive the past. I was afraid that we might become so involved in the daily demands of the world of work that we would break that thread of connection to generations of women before us. I greatly admire the way men seize the moment, take on the tasks of the day with single-minded purpose. But that is not for us; women have traditionally been multiple-minded. And so we still are, thank God. We, of course, do what the job — whatever it is — requires, but often with some other concern nagging at the backs of our brains.

Instead of this being some late-twentieth-century definition of life on the distaff side, I would argue that it's always been this way — that women have always played many roles at the same time. For years my mother kept telling me that it's nothing new to have women as soldiers, as diplomats, as politicians, as revolutionaries, as explorers, as founders of large institutions, as leaders in business, that the women of my generation did not invent the wheel. In the past women might not have had the titles, she painstakingly and patiently explained, but they did the jobs that fit those descriptions. Now I'm finally old enough, and have had enough life experience of my own, to listen to my mother. In her eighties, she maddeningly responds to almost all "new" developments with some similar story from the past, concluding with her favorite expression, *"Plus ça change, plus c'est la même chose."*

This little volume will attempt to tell some stories about the many roles women play, discovered both through my own life and the lives of other women. It involves no original research about women in history. I've learned about them from other people's work, usually in preparation for an event for some group like the Red Cross, or women state legislators, or Catholic schoolteachers. Interviews with living women came as part of my work as a reporter for ABC News and National Public Radio. And of course my own stories are just that — my own.

But I'm always struck by the similarity in women's stories, no matter how different they may superficially seem. That's because of the thread of continuity with women throughout the ages, the sense that we are doing what women have always done even as we pioneer our way across cultural divides or declare a revolution.

When we lived in Greece we used to go to the beach at Marathon. (We had to dodge the runners on the highway retracing the original race to Athens, blissfully unaware, it seems, that the man they were imitating dropped dead on arrival.) At first I marveled at the fact that we regularly went swimming at this place that I had read about in the history books ever since I was a little girl. Looking out to sea, I could imagine the frightening Persian fleet attacking, the brave Athenian soldiers defending their democracy. A great mound that was supposed to cover the Persian dead stood as a reminder of the oft-told tales of the courageous deeds of those long-ago men.

After we had been going to Marathon for a while, we found nestled in the hills another site, one that never made the history books but made me marvel more. It dated back thousands of years earlier than the famous battle, and a tiny museum had been erected to display the findings. Here was nothing of heroic dimensions, nothing on a grand scale: in one case, needles, buttons; in another, jewelry, pots for makeup; in another, frying pans and toys. Here the objects from the everyday lives of women from thousands of

years ago overwhelmed me with their famil-
iarity. I could have opened the cases, put on
their jewels, and taken up their tools, picked
up where they left off without a moment's
hesitation or confusion. What was left from
the lives of the men? Objects of war and
objects of worship, recognizable for soldiers
and priests, but what of the others? That
little museum has always symbolized for me
the great strength of women. We are connected throughout time and regardless of
place. We are our mothers' daughters.

SISTER

When my older sister died she was younger than I am now. Any woman who's been even slightly close to her big sister knows what that means — it means uncharted territory. It never occurred to me that this would happen, that I'd be on my own in a way that I never expected. Until Barbara died, it had never occurred to me that I had not been on my own. I had not realized, did not have a clue, how much I counted on her to do it first.

All of my life she had been there, lording it over me and loving me, pushing me around and protecting me. Those elusive early childhood memories that shimmer to the surface when summoned all involve her. Running to her when the dog next door jumped up and grabbed my two-year-old hair in its teeth. Barbara running to our mother complaining that if I insisted on putting on doll clothes, couldn't I be confined to the backyard. Going to school where she, four years older, shepherded me from room to room. Getting her out of classes to pull my baby teeth. Huddling together against the brother between us in age, the common enemy.

She excelled at everything, always. She was the president of the class, the school, the top student, the best writer, debater. She was also very beautiful. Every so often a thoughtless teacher would ask, why can't you be more like your sister? But I don't ever remember being jealous of her. I just desperately wanted to please her, and I often didn't. She had the ability to push all my buttons, the way most women (including my daughter) complain their mothers do. Because she was there between us, my mother and I never experienced the usual mother-daughter tensions. That gift lives on after her.

We had such a good time together that she once said, "If we lived next door to each other, we'd never go to work." It's true that I never laugh as hard as I do with the women in my family — my sister, mother, daughter. Fortunately for her community, I never lived next door and Barbara toiled tirelessly as a public servant taking painstaking care of everyone else until the day she died.

The dying part was so profound, and so profoundly weird, that it taught me a great deal about sisterhood, in all its meanings.

One fine day in October 1989 Barbara and I in our separate cities, unbeknownst to each other, went like responsible middle-aged ladies for our annual mammograms. In retrospect, it reminded me of the years when we lived in rooms next door to each other and would occasionally emerge at the same time humming the same bar of the same tune under our breaths. But this time nothing else was the same. The technician told me the usual "Check with us in a few days." The person who read the pictures of Barbara's breast clucked and sent her in for more X rays — her lungs, her liver, her bones, her brain. (She called these, plus the endless CT scans and MRIs that would come over the course of the next year, and that we carried from doctor to doctor, "The Inside Story of Barbara Sigmund.")

She phoned me the next morning. "I have cancer everywhere," she said. "You have to help me tell Mamma." I got off the phone and crumpled into Steven's arms. "We're going to lose her. Nobody has cancer that many places and lives," I sobbed. Her friend and neighbor, a radiologist, told her that without treatment she had perhaps six months to live. With treatment, who knew? Maybe miracles! She had turned fifty only a few months before.

We arranged for me to go to my mother's office at a free time in her schedule, and Barbara agreed to keep her phone free at that time. (Free times and free phones are rare in our family.) The plan was for me to be with Mamma while my sister told her the dread diagnosis. This was Barbara's attempt to correct what she thought was a bad mistake seven years before when she had reached Mamma alone at the end of a workday and blurted out that she had to have her eye removed. That, of course, should have served as a warning to us. But the doctor at the time told us that the chances of the melanoma behind her left eye recurring were less than if she had never had cancer at all. And Barbara handled the whole thing with such incredible style and panache, sporting spectacular sequined or feathered eye patches with evening dresses, matching an outfit with a color-coordinated patch for everyday wear. She never seemed sick, just understandably tired in the middle of her political campaigns, and the famous five-year mark for cancer patients had passed successfully.

The appointed hour with my mother came at about 11:30 in the morning. "Perfect," pronounced my Jewish husband, "you tell her and then the two of you go straight to

21

noon Mass." And that's what happened. Then began the pathetic odyssey of people living under the death sentence of widespread cancer. First, trying to get information, what were the treatments, where were they, what was the success rate? What we learned eventually, certainly not right away: When it comes to this highly experimental stuff, everybody's guessing.

After the initial terror, we settled into something of a routine. Barbara and her husband, Paul, would travel from their home in Princeton, New Jersey, to a hospital in Philadelphia. I would meet them there and spend the nights in her room, watching poison chemicals drip into my sister's body. Mamma would come up from Washington for most of the time as well. Then we would head back to Princeton and Mamma or I or my brother's wife, our other sister, would stay with Barbara until she was feeling better.

In those months, circles upon circles of sisters emerged. In the hospital, one of the doctors on Barbara's team was a woman whose willingness to tell us the truth was something I will forever value. It's not that the male doctors weren't caring; it's just that they couldn't deal with what they saw as their own failure, their inability to lick the disease. Another woman doctor, a pathologist who had nothing to do with the case, adopted Mamma and me when she saw us in the cafeteria. She would come visit in the room and cheer us up — yes, a cheery pathologist! — during her time "off." Then there were the legions of nurses, those sensible, funny, wonderful women who have the strength to deal with death on a daily basis.

Back in Princeton, the women of the town swung into action. Each gave according to her ability, to us who were so needy. People organized to cook and bring food, to visit, to run errands, to help with the mail that pours in when a public figure's illness is announced. And this for a full year! Most of the time Barbara kept working at her job as mayor, but the women in her office often had to take up the slack during the times she was in the hospital. With the attendant immune problems from chemotherapy, hospital stays became common for both of us as I took on the role of what Barbara called her "private duty sister." Again, there were a few fabulous men who gave of themselves completely, including their blood and, more important, their time. But my brother-in-law, the most giving and suffering of us all, noticed how it was women who kept Barbara and him going.

While these women tended to Barbara, others tended to Mamma and me. Our colleagues, busy professional women all, were incredibly attentive. The support systems and sisterhood of women working together had never been more important. My two closest friends arranged their vacation schedules to make sure that I would never be alone if I needed them, and they filled in the blanks that I was leaving at work without my even knowing about it. My mother's colleagues were members of Congress — talk about busy women! But they were there for her throughout that long year, and after Barbara died they came back from their campaigns, including several who were running for the Senate, to hold a private Mass in the Congresswomen's Reading Room at the Capitol (a room now named for my mother, the only room in the Capitol named for a woman).

Over the summer, as her condition deteriorated, the treatments stopped but better therapy arrived when Barbara's three boys came home. All in their early twenties then, they found ways to be in Princeton to the utter delight of their dying mother. When the fall came, and she waved them off, she knew she was seeing them for the last time.

Then it became time for the women to

gather around. And they did. The hair-dresser would come to the house and regale us with stories as she tried to keep Barbara's head beautiful above her sad, sick body. My daughter, Rebecca, in her junior year at Princeton University, became her aunt's nurse of choice in those final few weeks. The Religious of the Sacred Heart, the nuns who had taught us as children and were now our friends and contemporaries and confidantes, would come by with Holy Communion and hilarious conversation. A dear friend devoted herself full-time to Barbara, defining sister-hood by action, not the accident of blood. The oncologist, a woman, visited and ex-plained to us what to expect when Barbara died, an act of simple kindness that some-how helped. Barbara made it possible for us all to learn through her suffering, giving us mainly unspoken lessons in how to die with dignity. Some of her instructions were clearly spoken. She planned her funeral, making sure it would be right, not leaving it to chance, by which, I only half joked, she meant her family. "Let me introduce my-self," I would jest, "I am Chance." She also wrote bald, unsentimental poems about what she called "A Diary of a Fatal Illness" and lived until she saw them published and read at the local Arts Council. Some medical

25

schools now use her poetry to teach students about dying.

My mother had announced that she would resign from Congress at the end of her term. She didn't say it at the time, but she did it so she could be with Barbara. The cancer, with no respect for schedule, deprived Mamma of that opportunity. I had expected to take a leave of absence to care for my sister at the end — just give me a signal, I said to the doctors. They did, the day before she died. The next day, Barbara and I had a good laugh as I was combing her hair, which hadn't been colored in a while. "I think we're seeing your natural hair color for the first time since you were fifteen," I teased. But despite attempts at humor, my mother could hear a change in my voice on the telephone. She arrived that night and had a little visit before bedtime. Barbara died before morning.

The first time I picked up the phone to call her came in response to a story on page one of that day's *New York Times*. The subject: childbirth for post-menopausal women. The article dutifully reported the how, where, who, and when. But it left out what was for me, and I knew would be for her, the key question — why? She had a whole routine about how women she knew were producing their own grandchildren with these late-in-life babies. Ready to have a good giggle, I dialed her number before I remembered she wouldn't be there to share my astonishment. The shock of her absence made me feel very alone.

At some point during Barbara's illness I began preparing myself for a different vision of my old age. Without really thinking about it, I had always assumed we'd occupy adjacent rockers on some front porch, either literally or figuratively. Now one of those chairs would be empty. Intellectually I understood that. But every time some new thing happens that she's not here for, emotionally it hits me all over again — that sense of charting new territories without the map of my older sister.

And here's what I didn't expect at all — not only was I robbed of some part of my future, I was also deprived of my past. When a childhood memory needed checking, all my life I had simply run it by Barbara. Now there's no one to set me straight. My mother and brother can help some. My brother and I have, in fact, grown a good deal closer since our sister died; after all, without him, I would not only not have a sister, I would not be a sister. But Tommy didn't go to school with me, share a room with me, grow up female with me. Though I love him dearly, he is not my sister.

There it is. For all of the wonderful expressions of sisterhood from so many sources, for all of the support I both receive and provide, for all of the friendships I cherish, it's not the same. I only had one sister.

POLITICIAN

Why is it that many women loudly proclaim that they hate politics and politicians but are thrilled when a woman is elected to office? Logically, you'd think they would want women to stay away from something they see as tainted and tawdry. (This is definitely not my view — I'm one of those rare people who like and respect politicians, and I see them up close and personal.) But no, our guts tell us that it's better for us and better for politics if women participate. And if what you're interested in is government action on behalf of women and children, there's plenty of data to tell us our guts are right. Women in office make a difference, and with the power of the women's vote behind them, they make a huge difference.

First, let me disassociate myself, as the politicians would say, from the sentiments I've just described. I don't hate politics and politicians; in my case, it would mean hating my family and everything it stands for, and I most decidedly do not. My father, Hale Boggs, went to Congress before I was born, my mother was elected to fill his seat after he disappeared in an airplane over Alaska. My childhood home was filled with politicians my entire life — they were friends, courtesy "uncles," fascinating storytellers, dedicated public servants, and a few genuine wackos. As children, my brother and sister and I thought of people like Sam Rayburn, Lyndon Johnson, Hubert Humphrey, and Gerald Ford as family friends who would come by for a casual dinner from the garden. We knew a lot of women who were politically active, our mother chief among them, but we didn't know many women in office. My sister-in-law Barbara, Tommy's wife, whom I've known since before I was born and for whom the suffix "in-law" seems ridiculous, worked as a new bride for Julia Butler Hansen, congresswoman from Washington. But by and large in my experience women were behind the scenes in politics, doing most of the work and getting none of the glory. My mother organized voter registration drives, traveled the country making speeches, advancing candidates, organizing rallies in every presidential election of her adult life. She ran my father's campaigns, organized his offices, presided over political institutions in Washington. During the years she did her stint as a congressional wife, neither the Democrats nor the Republicans pushed women to get involved either as candidates or as voters. Politicians had decided there was no such thing as the "women's vote."

Bear with me here for a little history. After the long push for women's suffrage finally succeeded in 1920 (don't you love the way history books say, "And then women got the right to vote," like it happened overnight?), the men in Congress got scared. They figured this new group of voters would demand all kinds of legislation to help women and children, so they introduced more than one hundred bills to do just that. The debate over the first federal measure dealing with health care, the Sheppard-Towner Act, made the cause and effect stunningly clear. We better do this, said supporters of the legislation designed to provide maternal and child health education, or the newly enfranchised women will punish us. The measure passed in 1921, and no one was punished. But no one was rewarded either. The politicians saw no payback at the polls. Women had pushed for the vote in order to bring about social reforms, but when politicians took the first tentative steps toward enacting the kind of change women wanted, they were greeted with silence from the ladies' gallery.

The promise, or threat, of the women's vote had failed to materialize.

Many women didn't vote at all, after working so hard for the right, and those who did, voted no differently from men. So the politicians soon lost interest. When the Sheppard-Towner Act came up for renewal in 1928, it was defeated. And in the 1930s, Depression-era laws were downright hostile to women. The Federal Economic Act of 1932 made it illegal for the wives of federal employees to hold government positions, and required that the wives of employed men be the first on the lists for firing. Overnight, fifteen hundred women lost their jobs. The National Recovery Act of 1935 made it the law that women working in government would receive 25 percent less pay than men doing the same jobs. It took almost thirty years to right that wrong.

So began a pattern repeated several times in the short political history of American women — expectations raised, then dashed as women failed to deliver at the ballot box. In the early days of public-opinion polling, the most common answer from women to questions about their views on public policy issues: "Wait until my husband gets home." Still, women's organizations — the League of Women Voters, Business and Professional

Women, the American Association of University Women, the YWCA — women in labor unions, and women in political parties kept up the pressure on politicians throughout the 1930s, 1940s, and 1950s, working for better health and safety, against child labor, and for equal pay.

Suddenly, in the 1960s, their efforts started paying off. The Equal Pay Act for government passed in 1963 (it had first been introduced in 1945!), followed the next year by the single most important law affecting women as workers — the 1964 Civil Rights Act. That's actually a funny story. The old curmudgeonly warhorse Howard Smith of Virginia tried desperately to kill the landmark law. He knew the bill banning racial discrimination was barreling down the track following Martin Luther King's march on Washington, President Kennedy's assassination, and President Johnson's dramatic "We Shall Overcome" speech before a joint session of Congress. So Smith cooked up a little mischief. His colleagues might be crazy enough, in his view, to end legal discrimination on the basis of race, but they certainly wouldn't go for anything that outlawed discrimination against women. Hoping to divide his opponents and bring down the bill, Smith added the word *sex* to the employment section of the bill. But the old man guessed wrong. There was no derailing civil rights that year and Democratic and Republican women in Congress maneuvered to keep the word *sex* in the bill up to the very end. Much to his dismay, Howard Smith's little plot made it illegal for employers to ever again say, "We don't hire women to do that."

When I graduated from college in June 1964, I heard that miserable sentence all the time, and it made me crazy, but there was nothing I could do about it. By the end of the summer, I would have grounds for a lawsuit. Of course, most employers didn't know that, and young women like me would have never acted on our newfound right. But many other women did. Throughout the 1960s, women sued and won against hundreds of companies that refused to hire or promote women. And a new women's political movement got going as well, putting the heat on Congress again to pay attention to women's issues. In 1972 more legislation passed than in the previous ten years combined — including the first federal child care act and the act banning discrimination in education, including sports. That measure, called Title IX, had the effect of creating a whole generation of women athletes. Then came equal credit, which had the effect of creating a whole generation of female business owners.

Why did all this legislation finally pass? What happened to turn Congress around after its disillusionment with women as a political force? Women's lives had changed, that's what happened. Women were graduating from college, having fewer babies, and getting divorced in numbers never known before. And what did that mean? It meant women in the workplace. And what did they find there? Glaring — and legal — inequality. For a long time, women just accepted their second-class status as inevitable, that's the way things were, there was nothing to be done about it. But then women started talking to each other, and then they started organizing. And when they came to Congress with their complaints they found a few female souls ready to listen, and act.

When the first woman, Republican Jeannette Rankin, was elected to Congress in 1917, she carried with her from the wilds of Montana a full bag of female concerns. Keep in mind, she was elected from one of the few states that allowed women to vote, so her first task, of course, was pushing for national suffrage. She also worked for women's health education (what became the Sheppard-Towner Act), against child labor, and for the establishment of child care centers for working mothers — this in 1918! As World War I heated up, the sole congresswoman militated for equal job opportunities and pay for women in war-related industries. But she also militated against war, and her highly unpopular vote opposing war against Germany cost her her seat. Rankin was defeated at the end of one term. (Years later, in 1940, just before World War II, Jeannette Rankin returned to Congress, again voted against the declaration of war, and again served only one term.)

Over the next few decades, women dribbled into Congress, many of them the widows of congressmen. Most arrived with no agenda for women in mind, but they all found, once they started serving, that women all over the country came to them with their concerns. When you call the roll of women who came to Congress in the twenties, thirties, forties, and fifties you find that they toiled in the corridors and the cloakrooms of the Capitol pressing their colleagues on equal pay, tax relief for single parents and working mothers, school lunches, consumer safety, food stamps, and the place of women in the military.

Equally important, they came to the table of government with different sensibilities.

Women simply experience life differently from men. And these mothers, sisters, daughters, and wives brought the perspectives of those roles to governing. When my mother was elected to Congress in 1973, she had just learned firsthand that many widows lost their credit along with their mates. It was bad enough to lose my father, who disappeared in an airplane over Alaska and was never found. He was Majority Leader of the House of Representatives at the time. To add insult to sorrow, Mamma found herself dealing with banks and creditors, trying to explain her peculiar situation. After an extensive and futile search for Daddy, when the time came to declare his seat vacant, no one questioned that Mamma was the best person for the congressional seat. And, as she remembers it, when the governor called the election, she responded like an old warhorse without ever thinking about it. My sister, a politician herself, told Mamma that the hardest part of her job would be voting. She was so used to smoothing things over for my father, acting as a go-between among the factions, that she would have a hard time declaring herself, coming down on one side versus the other. As Barbara told her, "Mamma, there's no 'maybe' button."

That was hard for her. But service on the

Banking and Currency Committee was not. It became a perfect place to right the wrongs of the credit discrimination she and friends of hers whose husbands had died or deserted them had experienced. As my mother tells the story, the committee was considering legislation barring banks from denying anyone a loan because of race, national origin, or creed. According to Mamma, she snuck into a back room, wrote the words "or sex or marital status" in longhand into the text of the bill, made copies, and then brought them back to her colleagues, saying in her sweet, southern way, "I'm sure the omission of women was just an oversight on your part." It helps to have a woman in the right place at the right time.

A few years later, Steve and I bought my mother's house (or evicted her, as she jokingly put it; at least I think she was joking), and she moved downtown to a condominium. It seemed to be taking an inordinately long time to get her loan approved, so she called the bank and said, "I find it passing strange that I haven't gotten my mortgage, and since my assets and income are a matter of public record, I have to assume that it's because I'm female and elderly. As an author of the equal credit bill, that concerns me." Needless to say, she got her loan that afternoon. Several years after that, when I was refinancing the house, the lawyer was shoving pieces of paper in front of me to sign. "What's this one?" I asked. "Oh, that's nothing," he replied, "it just says that we didn't discriminate against you on the basis of sex, age, or race." "That's not nothing," I sternly retorted, "that's my mother's legislation."

If it helps to have a woman in the right place at the right time, it helps even more if that woman is backed by millions of women voters who might retaliate politically — throw the bums out, or in. That's what the politicians worried about back in the 1920s. Finally, in 1980, sixty years after suffrage, they had reason to worry. In that election, for the first time women turned out to vote in the same proportion as men and they voted differently from men. Thus was born the now famous gender gap, which has become such a fixture in American politics. There's a lot of confusion about the term *gender gap*. It does not mean that women vote for women. It's simply a description of the difference between the way men and women vote. In that election a majority of the men and a majority of the women voted for Ronald Reagan, but women did so by a smaller percentage than men did. The space between those percentages was christened the "gender gap."

The fact that women had voted differently stirred up a good deal of interest among politicians — but nowhere near as much interest as they showed two years later. Then women, who turned out to vote in greater numbers than men, managed to elect politicians who lost the male vote. If the election that year had been reserved for men only, Mario Cuomo would not have been governor of New York, Jim Blanchard would not have been governor of Michigan, and twenty-six Republicans who lost their seats in the House of Representatives would have probably kept them. Women stirred by the recession, as the last hired first fired, and upset about threats to Social Security, where they make up the bulk of recipients, voted against Republicans. And boy did the politicians take notice!

It was as if a spotlight suddenly shone on everyone in a skirt in Congress. Men rushed to join the Congressional Caucus on Women's Issues. They followed the lead of the congresswomen in passing a passel of bills helping women and children: public service jobs, a crackdown on domestic violence, pension reform, and child support enforcement. Some of those bills had been hanging around for decades, but the congresswomen took the newfound power of the women's vote onto the floors of the House and Senate and worked across party lines to get the legislation passed. Republican women were invited for regular sessions at the White House where they were asked to give tutorials on "what women want." What a heady time it was for women politicians! So much so that Democrats decided to put a woman on the presidential ticket — hoping that would give them some small shot at ousting Ronald Reagan. Women around the country cheered for the first female in the second spot, but they didn't vote for her. The majority still went for Reagan and Bush over Mondale and Ferraro. And the day after the 1984 election, when the Democrats had lost forty-nine states, the politicians once again started focusing all their attention on the white male vote.

So it happened again. Expectations raised, expectations dashed. But this time, even though politicians lost interest in women, there was no going back to the old days. Two things had changed since the 1930s: one, the women's vote elected four United States senators who lost the male vote in 1984; and two, there were enough women in Congress determined to keep pressing for their agenda.

Let's take a moment here to explain what the women's vote is, and what it is not. It is not a vote based on abortion. All of our polling tells us that men and women vote exactly the same on that issue. The women's vote is an economic vote. Women not only make less money than men, they are also much more likely to be the beneficiaries of government programs, or the caretakers of beneficiaries. That's particularly true of Social Security and Medicare (we wish men lived as long as we do, but they don't), but it's also true of food stamps and welfare. Women also often work for government-funded institutions — schools, nursing homes, hospitals, day care centers, museums, social services offices. So women tend to be less wary of government than many men are, and that makes women more likely to vote for the Democratic Party's candidate.

Both parties hate the fact that, all things being equal, the women's vote goes Democratic — Republicans for the very sensible reason that it means the majority of voters go for the opposition party; Democrats worry that it means real men don't like Democrats. And there's a lot of truth to that. But both parties also know that they need the women's vote to win elections.

Because of that the women in Congress managed through the 1980s to drip their issues over their colleagues' heads like a Chinese water torture. Drip, child care, drip, child support enforcement, drip, mammography coverage by Medicare, drip, increased funding for breast cancer research, drip, commercial credit for women. It's not that the men don't care about those issues, it's just that they don't put them at the top of their priority lists the way women do. And the congresswomen organized across party lines, consciously placing their members on as many committees as possible, in order to keep up the pressure for their programs. But it was tough because there were so few of them, never more than twenty-nine in the House, two in the Senate.

Every election, we women in the press would write hopefully that this was the Year of the Woman. The results embarrassed us over and over again. Finally, in 1992, it came true. After that election, forty-seven women went to the House, eight to the Senate. What a moment! It seemed like women were everywhere all of a sudden, even though the percentages were still tiny. For the first time it was possible to measure statistically what we knew instinctively — that women in office make a difference on key issues. That's been tracked in the state legislatures for years, but there were never enough women at the national level to be able to say it with certainty. One good example: gun control. Women see this as a "mommy issue" — no machine guns on playgrounds, good idea! The ban on assault weapons would have never passed Congress had there been fewer women in 1993. Only 23 percent of Republican men voted for it, but 67 percent of Republican women did. On the Democratic side, 89 percent of the women voted to get rid of the high-powered guns, compared with 72 percent of the men. It was a close vote where women made the difference.

The American political scene is so volatile, and we in the media are so ready to look for something new to characterize each election, that the 1992 Year of the Woman quickly gave way to the 1994 focus on "the angry white male" and then the 1996 "soccer mom." Each was an attempt to describe key voters in those elections and they reflect the ups and downs of women on the political scene. But in each election women held their own in Congress and the increased numbers of Republican women meant their voices were heard in party counsels. Because of the concerted effort of those congresswomen, Republicans included a strong child support enforcement section in the welfare reform bill.

And for anyone who doubted the power of the women's vote in 1996, the party conventions said it all. I often get a giggle at the thought of the ghosts of the old pols of the past hovering in the rafters of those convention halls, celestial cigars clenched in their teeth, puzzling over what all those women were doing on the podium, talking about the problems of coping with work and children. Hillary Clinton even threw in the difficulty of getting the dog to the vet. Bob Dole was trailing so badly among women in the polls that Republicans in Congress labored to shore up their own female support and passed a bundle of bills to do just that. Since two-thirds of the people who earn a minimum wage are women, they voted to increase the minimum wage. They also expanded health care coverage, mandated to insurance companies that they cover at least a forty-eight-hour hospital stay for new mothers (to put an end to what the president so elegantly called "drive-by deliveries"), and they added domestic violence to the list of crimes that would make a person ineligible for gun ownership. And it worked. Republicans held on to Congress while women voted overwhelmingly Democratic for president. Had women's suffrage never been enacted, Bob Dole would be president today.

That puts women in the enviable position of having both parties vie for their attention. The first bill introduced in the new Congress was one allowing workers to choose between time off and more money when they put in extra hours, and it was aimed directly at working women. With fifty women now in the House and nine in the Senate, it's much harder for women's concerns to fall in the cracks. So there's good news here. There's even more good news when you look at what's happening in the states. In the years since 1969 the percentage of women in the state legislatures has grown from 4 percent to almost 22 percent. That's important both because the states serve as farm teams for the national legislature — 94 percent of the women now in Congress served before this in some other office — and because the women in local legislatures protect the interests of families and children as more programs devolve from the federal government to the states.

Women have now knocked over every political barrier except president and vice president. One of the last to fall was state attorney general. Voters just didn't seem ready to elect a woman as the chief law enforcement officer. Finally, in 1984, Arlene Violet, a

Republican woman in Rhode Island leaped that hurdle. I was terribly interested in what had happened in the smallest state to give it the courage to elect "General Violet." Then I discovered that Arlene Violet had been a nun, and though voters might not be comfortable turning over law enforcement to a woman, they had no problem putting a nun in charge of disciplining the society.

What about a woman president? That's the question I'm always asked. Will it happen in my lifetime? I suppose it depends on how long I live. There are now many women in place, women who could be credibly chosen for the number one or two spot on a national ticket. It's more likely for the Republicans to make that move than the Democrats, as they have more to gain by making a gesture toward the ladies since they have so much trouble with the women's vote. Even though Republican women don't usually win the majority of the votes of their own sex, they can cut into a Democratic candidate's hold on the women's vote enough to get elected. In truth, I think it's likely that the first woman president will be a vice president who comes to office because of the misfortune — natural or otherwise — of a male president. As long as we don't organize to do him in, that's okay with me.

CONSUMER ADVOCATE

"Esther Peterson, a dogged consumer advocate whose work has an impact on Americans every time they buy a can of soup or a box of laundry detergent, died today at her home in Washington. She was 91." That was the lead of the obituary in *The New York Times* at the end of 1997. The story behind those words is one of the great tales of an American woman in the twentieth century.

Through much of the time I was growing up in Washington, Esther Peterson was a fixture on the political scene, pitching in for various Democratic administrations, participating in activities at the Women's National Democratic Club, where my mother presided in some years, and spent a good deal of time and energy in others. When I returned to town as a reporter in 1977, I found Mrs. Peterson working the corridors of Congress as President Carter's consumer advocate. Her trademark braid wrapped around her head, she marched through the Capitol with a wide grin at the ready, always taking time to greet me even in the middle of an earnest appeal to a recalcitrant lawmaker. I kept looking for an excuse to sit down with her for a lengthy interview. She kept asking me the subject matter, and when I said, "Esther Peterson," she put me off until she had more time.

Finally, in 1993, I got my chance. She was eighty-seven years old and back in government with the latest Democratic administration, this time as a representative to the United Nations. *This week with David Brinkley* had decided to scrap the usual format for the Christmas program and all of us regulars interviewed someone we found interesting. I chose Esther Peterson.

She started her story with her grandmothers, both converted to Mormonism in Denmark. Both made the daring and dangerous passage across the ocean and across the country to Utah. One was part of the Mormon pilgrimage that trekked over the plains. The fact that she took such inspiration from what she called "the inheritance of strength" struck a special chord with me. Whenever I hear modern women complain that they "can't do it all," I think of those women who went on foot across this continent, bearing and burying babies, spinning cloth for clothes, creating meals out of nothing, then settling in a place where they had to chop, plow, plant, build to have a home and a livelihood. They never insisted they couldn't be superwomen. Their experiences provided the context for Esther Peterson's childhood world.

Then there was her mother. One of the first women to attend what was then Brigham Young Academy, her mother was forced to go to work running an old folks' home when her father, the superintendent of schools, became ill. Those many years later her still-proud daughter told me, "She held the family together, economically. There's no doubt about it. But she was a woman." That was Esther Peterson's explanation of how she came to do what she did. How she came to dedicate her life to educating women so that they could improve their lives and those of their families.

As with many women, hers was anything but a straight path. First, she had to make her own daring journey — to New York City to graduate school at Columbia Teachers College, unheard of for a good Mormon girl and strongly opposed by her mother because her father had just died and her duty was to be by her mother's side. Esther Peterson's solution? She took her mother with her to New York, where the older woman lasted for about a week and then went home. "But

I think I did the right thing" — she was still questioning her decision sixty years later — "it was a matter of encompassing, rather than closing doors, which is something I felt strongly about for a long time in my life."

One of the doors that opened was held by Oliver Peterson, whom she describes as a pipe-smoking socialist — two strikes against him in Mormon Utah. But they married and moved to Boston where she, like other well-brought-up young women, taught at a posh girls' school and like most women, especially Mormon women, also did volunteer work. It was through that most traditional of paths that Esther Peterson became a labor activist and then a consumer advocate.

She volunteered as a teacher at the YWCA teaching working girls in the evening. One night when she walked into a nearly empty classroom, Mrs. Peterson learned that her students were on strike, walking the picket line. Their boss had changed the shape of the pockets on the housedresses they made from a square, easy to sew on, to a heart, much more difficult and time-consuming. Since they were paid by the dress, this slowed them down and resulted in less pay for more work. More than five decades later, Esther Peterson remembered her reaction: "I thought a strike was simply terrible. I was raised you had bombs in your pockets and you were communists. But Oliver said, 'Go find out. Go find out.' He was wonderful. And I went and saw industrial homework for the first time. I saw what it meant when the whole family sat around one electric light bulb. I shan't forget it. And I asked about the strike, and I heard about it. So the next morning, I went out, and I was on the picket line and helped them."

That was the beginning. The working women won what came to be called the Heartbreaker strike with the help of others organized by Esther Peterson into the Citizens' Committee of Concerned Women. They put on their best finery and stood in the picket line intimidating the Boston police. "Then I became a real labor activist," Mrs. Peterson recalled. "I decided they had to have a voice, the working people. I felt the women were left out, they got the low end of everything, you see. And that was important to me."

So, it was women she organized. First, it was teachers in Massachusetts. Then it was garment workers in New York where she moved for her husband's job. It was World War II, and white women were moving into better factory jobs as black women moved from domestic work into the lower jobs the white women left behind. As Esther Peterson went around signing them up for the union, she often brought her toddler daughter with her, showing them that she had the same problems with child care they did.

When Oliver Peterson's job moved them to Washington, D.C., his wife became a lobbyist for the Amalgamated Clothing Workers. A female lobbyist for a union in the 1940s! This was the Washington of smoke-filled rooms and snuff-filled spittoons. According to Mrs. Peterson, the CIO chief took one look at her and said, " 'What the hell do we do with Esther?' In those days they assigned each person to a congressman or a senator. They said, 'Give her to Kennedy, he won't amount to anything.' And I tell you, my dear, that was the best break I ever had." She and the future president became fast friends, something that would serve her well in later years.

All this time, while organizing the work force, Esther Peterson was also producing a family. Briefly after the birth of her first child she stayed at home but found herself depressed, and her husband urged her to get back to work. When she wrote her memoirs in the last years of her life, she dedicated the book "to those who are often forgotten, but who have allowed me to enjoy my life as well as my work — my housekeepers, my babysitters, and of course, my family." While pregnant with her fourth child, she was lobbying for an increase in the minimum wage. Senator Claude Pepper told her, "Esther, if it's a boy we'll call it Maxie for maximum hours, if it's a girl we'll call it Minnie for minimum wage." "So you were not only a female lobbyist for a labor union, you were a pregnant female?" I asked incredulously. "You know the thing is that women can do things," came the answer. "Women can do things if they want to and the men didn't mind my bulge."

Despite her success in the labor movement, Mrs. Peterson was always ready to pick up and go when her husband's job summoned them. That's the kind of thing I think young women often get tied up in knots about, and where her example's useful. Given the life span of most women, we can expect to be in the work force for decades, if that's what we choose. It makes a lot of sense to me to take advantage of new situations when they present themselves, even if it means taking some time out from a career for a while. It made sense to Esther Peterson as well. So when the State Department asked Oliver Peterson to go to Sweden as a labor attaché in 1948, she didn't hesitate. "Wherever we've gone, I've found good, interesting things to do. And I knew that would happen here too. And it was a new opportunity. I thought it was simply splendid. Why not?"

In Sweden she learned that domestic workers were covered by labor laws establishing hours, work conditions, and pay. She contacted the Women's Bureau at the U.S. Department of Labor, which asked her to do a study of the Swedish system. Though she was disappointed in how the government handled her report, she marveled at the Swedish system, particularly the job of "mother substitute" — someone to take on the mother's role when she is not able. In her memoir, *Restless*, Peterson says of this job, "It was a great way for middle-aged women who didn't work full-time to make a little extra money and to feel useful. It was a way of assigning value to women's traditional skills. It was an inspiring use of the talents and resources of older women. It was so refreshing to see the recognition of the social and economic value of 'women's work.' " Half a century has passed and still nothing similar exists here.

Her old union buddies asked Mrs. Peterson to go to London for the International Confederation of Free Trade Unions in

1949, where she was the only female in the U.S. delegation. "Did you find that lonely?" I asked her. "No, I'd always liked men and got along with them. And I think they liked me. You know, I'd give them credit." What a familiar story. My mother always said that you could get anything done as long as you didn't have to get the credit. Not an easy maxim for a politician, but useful.

When the Petersons returned to the United States in 1957, after Esther had established the first international summer school for working women, she returned to the Amalgamated Clothing Workers where the union tried to pay her two thousand dollars less than the man who had just left the job. The explanation? Your husband has a job. Needless to say, this woman who had worked her whole adult life for fairness for working women wouldn't accept injustice when it came to her own situation. She fought the union and won. But quickly her interests turned to the presidential campaign of her old friend Jack Kennedy, where she put her formidable organizing skills to work.

With victory came the spoils, somewhat to her embarrassment. As she recounted the conversation with President Kennedy, "He said, 'What do you want?' And I thought, 'My land, what do I want?' My husband was quite ill and I wouldn't leave Washington. So I said, 'Well, the Women's Bureau because I'm interested in women's affairs.' And that's how that developed." What's more, she convinced the president to establish a Commission on the Status of Women, an idea that had been kicked around Congress for a decade. And she persuaded President Kennedy to ask Eleanor Roosevelt to chair the commission, despite Mrs. Roosevelt's support for Adlai Stevenson for the presidential nomination.

As the commission went around the country gathering information, Peterson used the pulpit of the Women's Bureau to preach to young women about the need to support themselves and to get a decent education. She caught a lot of flak for her efforts, and critics accused her of luring women away from home and hearth, but she learned a lot as well. "I remember going through factories. And I'll never forget one of them, Bendix. Here was this rather puny little man, and a woman was next to him, and she was lifting the thing down onto the conveyor belt. And I said, 'Isn't that his job?' 'He's too small, he can't do it.' And she was paid less than he was."

The commission pushed for equal pay for women, and when the bill passed it was a great moment for Esther Peterson. "One of the last bills that President Kennedy signed was the Equal Pay Bill, 1963. I'm selfish. I call it my bill. I worked awfully hard and the secretary [of Labor] said, 'Oh, Esther, equal pay, come on.' I said, 'Well, can I try?' and they said, 'If you do, we'll have nothing to do with it.' Nothing could have been better because I wanted to lobby it myself and we got it through." The commission also managed to end job designation by sex in the civil service and attacked the issue of property rights for married women. Keep in mind what the laws were in 1963. Some states gave husbands complete control of their wives' earnings, some prohibited direct inheritance by married women, some forbade women to go into business for themselves without the permission of the court. (It was not until 1980 that the U.S. Census Bureau broadened the "head of household" definition to include women.) Just laying this stuff out for all the world to see made a difference.

It also made a difference that Esther Peterson became assistant secretary of labor for labor standards, making her the highest-ranking woman in government in 1963. (This doesn't say a lot for John F. Kennedy; Dwight Eisenhower had a female in his cabinet.) Even so, she found herself excluded from some meetings she was entitled to attend, and in the spirit of the times, simply took it. She found herself being forced to take a lot over the next few years, after President Johnson created the Consumer Affairs Bureau and named her as the first director. As soon as the president announced her job, the letters from irate customers started pouring in at the rate of about a hundred and fifty a day. But she found that there was no real commitment to this cause in the White House, that she had no staff and no budget. So what did she do? Called on women to volunteer to help her — the League of Women Voters, the Consumers League, and the American Association of University Women — to sort through the mail by subject matter. And then she took on the tough topics of food labels and packaging.

"Oh, and my, the way they went after me," she said with a laugh thirty years later. "Some of the food manufacturers were saying, 'You're taking the romance out of marketing,' and I remember I said, 'I know lots of better places for romances than the aisles of a supermarket.'" But she saw her battles for what eventually became truth in packaging, truth in advertising, and truth in lending legislation as a continuation of her lifelong interest in educating women to improve their lives. None of it was popular with the business community, or with many members of the Johnson administration, and in the end she was forced out of the executive office building and back into the arms of her labor union. There she tried to bring her consumer-friendly ideas to the union cooperative stores and met nothing but hidebound opposition. Much to her surprise, this woman who had spent her life taking on business interests found a home in private industry.

The Giant Food supermarket chain had listened long enough to her talk about ingredients and labeling and freshness, complaints that essentially came out of her own role as the family's shopper. As she told the story, the management came to her with the message "Put up or shut up" and offered her a job as consumer representative. She made a deal that she would do things her way and if the stores ran into trouble as a result, she would quit. Giant thrived on the goodwill created by Esther Peterson's institution of a consumer bill of rights, freshness dating, unit pricing, ingredient labeling — all long before these things were required by law. Mrs. Peterson asked the questions any shopper wanted answered, like what does it mean when the fish department labels its wares "fresh" and "fancy"? "What's a fancy fish?" asked the new consumer representative. "Well, it's one that's been previously frozen," came back the answer. "So I said, 'Why don't you say so?' 'Oh, no one will buy it.' So I said, 'Then we have a consumer bill of rights except for the fish department.'" That exchange had the effect of correcting the labels, and still the store sold fish. Just give women the information, Mrs. Peterson insisted, and they can make intelligent decisions.

She learned a few home truths about the absurdity of some government regulations as she put in years at Giant, and tried to take them back to government when the Democrats returned to power and President Carter asked her to come back, at the age of seventy-one, to serve as his consumer advocate. This time her main job was to see to the passage of legislation creating a consumer agency as a government department. The seasoned lobbyist was horrified at the inexperience and arrogance of the new administration, and not surprised when the legislation failed. But she was able to work with the heads of regulatory agencies to establish energy efficiency labels and fuel economy ratings, a practical response to the energy shortage of the era. She also accomplished some consumer protections for airplane passengers and in the funeral home industry, where she unfortunately shared the customer's experience when her beloved Oliver died in 1979. Throughout all those years, from the time of the Kennedy administration, while she was working for the American consumer she was also caring for her husband, tending him through his long illness.

As he left office, President Carter presented Esther Peterson with the highest-ranking civilian honor — the medal of freedom. It seemed a fitting end to a long life of service. But neither the return of Republican rule nor her advancing age stopped her activism. She pushed for an international list of banned products as a representative of the International Consumers Union at the United Nations. Once again she was the butt of much criticism from the business community as she tried to let developing nations know that some of the products coming from America were considered unsafe in this country. I asked how her family handled the attacks. "I think sometimes, 'Oh, Mama, do you have to yell so much?' And especially during the time when I was in the newspaper a lot, 'Oh, Mama, come on.' But they were kind, they knew me for what I am. They said, 'You can't change Mama. She's like she is.' " Thank goodness. What a model. Here was a woman who essentially took the traditional role of teacher and trainer and shopper and used it to make the lives of thousands of women and their families better. And she kept it up until the very end.

When the Democrats came back in with Bill Clinton, she was appointed as a representative to the United Nations, where she told me she saw positive movement in the international organization which seemed to most of us to be headed for disaster. "I'm encouraged," she declared in the face of all odds. "But," I protested, "you have spent your life being encouraged." To which this lovely old warrior replied, "Why give up, my dear? One never does, one never should. Wouldn't it be dismal?"

AUNT

"Aunts are great," chirped my then seven-year-old niece recently. The proximate cause of this utterly satisfying statement was a gummy dinosaur just purchased by me at the Museum of Natural History. It was at the end of a morning of many adventures, including subway rides, a visit to the new exhibition, and the offer that she and her twin sister could buy any "little" thing they wanted at the museum store. For me, it was special time spent with two fascinating characters whose behavior is not my responsibility. For them, it was a chance to command my undivided attention, to be blissfully "spoiled." A few weeks later, it was a great-niece's turn. She had just turned four and I had promised her, as my godchild, a day with just the two of us. No big sister, no baby brother. Just us. For this act of true friendship, as far as she's concerned, I am regularly rewarded with the most scrumptious of hugs and referred to as her "fairy godmother."

The relationship to an adult not your parent can be one of the best in life. Aunts, uncles, grandparents, great-aunts and -uncles, courtesy aunts, and uncles — all made such a difference in my life, and in the lives of my own children. Now I find that the same is true in the other direction — that nieces and nephews, great-nieces and -nephews, and friends' children make my life richer and fuller. And, of course, I can't wait for grandchildren. (I'm trying to keep my cool on this subject, but my kids aren't exactly in the dark about my feelings.)

When I was growing up we lived part of the year in New Orleans, part of the year in Washington, so it had the feel of a somewhat schizophrenic childhood. In Louisiana, I was surrounded by family. My mother was an only child, but her mother sometimes lived next door with two of her sisters and their mother. Six blocks away was my mother's first cousin Shingo, not an actual aunt, but considered one, what we call a "tante." Her daughters were just on either side of me in age. Though I found my own house fascinating with its mix of politicos from all parts of town and every ethnic background, it was sometimes a relief to skip the six safe blocks to a world with backyard swings and midday snacks. I loved stuffing envelopes at our dining room table with the campaign volunteers; it made me feel wonderfully competent to be able to fold the election flyers with the best of them. And I listened avidly to all the conversation about issues and intrigue. But it was also nice to listen as Shingo read children's stories, to go from tales of huge corruption to ones about high cockalorum. During one really rough campaign, even though her house was under construction and there was a new baby, I moved in with Shingo for most of the summer.

Various other relatives were always around. On any given night at my great-aunt Rowena's next door, twelve to fourteen people would gather around the dinner table, all related to me in some way that they would carefully explain if I couldn't get out of the way fast enough. Sometimes I would make the mistake of asking my mother or grandmother who some "stranger" was. That would evoke the lengthy genealogical discourse that southern families so love. My children correctly accuse me of the same sin.

My father's mother and father, about an hour and a half away on the Mississippi Gulf Coast, had a house on a big family compound, along with several of their children. In the summer, I would spend weeks at a time there, going from one house to the next, but mainly staying with my aunt Tootsie who had seven children of her own and didn't seem to mind a few more. (She's still that way now, even in her eighties.) My aunts and my grandmother would tell my sister, brother, our cousins, and me stories of their childhood, and my father's. We loved to listen to any tales that revealed him as a less than perfect child. His sisters were happy to lovingly oblige. Now several of my cousins who are my contemporaries have houses on the property and it's great fun to go back and tell each other's kids about all the outlaw things we did, like sneaking out to the beach at night or smoking under the bayou bridge.

In Washington, unless some family member was visiting, which wasn't unusual, it was our parents' friends and, later, our friends' parents who were the meaningful grown-ups in our lives (other than our teachers and the housekeeper who ruled us). Because so many people move to the capital from someplace else, friends often become family in Washington even more so than in other places. And I think my parents' friends had grown especially close during World War II, when many of the men were away and the women banded together to pool the ration coupons and provide the moral support. We lived in a neighborhood where we were in and out of each other's houses, and someone else's mother was just as likely to take care of you as your own. My "aunt" Lizzie had the surest hand with the scissors so she had the task of trimming my bangs and hemming my skirts. As we grew older, nearly all of my friends' grandmothers moved in with them. They would often help us with the costumes and cookies for school plays and bake sales, regaling us with stories of "the olden days" while we stitched and stirred.

At a party my parents gave for Lynda Johnson's wedding, President Johnson talked about how important it was for him to have befriended his father's friends and how important it was for his children to know his friends. It was a lovely sentiment, but it's the mothers and daughters whose friendships have lasted. Mrs. Johnson and my mother still take vacations together, and Lynda and I have inherited their friendship. Lynda's daughter, Lucinda, and my Becca are friends, but Lucinda was an even better friend of my sister, Barbara. And she feels close to my mother as well.

The men in this universe of adults often charmed and delighted us, but they were mostly drop-ins on our lives. It was the women we spent time with, it was from them that we learned about other generations, about how things used to be, and how things would forever be. My mother's mother and aunts were quite a group. My mother refers to them as flappers, but by the time I knew them well that era had passed. When I first became conscious of this sisterhood, each was on her second husband. For a while three of them, and a half sister, plus my mother were all married to men whose last names began with *B*. My mother loves to tell the story of the *B* handkerchiefs, given one Christmas by one of my great-aunts to my great-uncle Hewitt Bouanchaud. His wife, my great-aunt Eustatia, oohed and aahed over them and then quickly disappeared with them to be rewrapped for the next Christmas and passed on to my great-aunt Frosty Blackshear's husband. Well, the same thing happened again, with each wife wrapping the handkerchiefs on each successive year until they went all the way around the family. Finally, they ended up in Hewitt's pile again. Much to the horror of the women he declared, "These handkerchiefs have been given to every man in the family, starting with me. This year I'm keeping them." And he proceeded to stuff them in his pocket out of reach of Eustatia. It wasn't easy to get out of Eustatia's reach. She was a fun-loving, piano-playing presence. She composed ragtime songs that she played with the *rat-a-tat* of her long fingernails on the keyboard. One involved her stamping out a couple of chords with her foot and then banging out the finale with her rear end on the ivories.

Then the second husbands all died and the great-aunts set off in active pursuit of husbands number three. (Only my grandmother succeeded in this quest.) Their attempts to "vamp" men were something to behold, and they would bring us in on the fabulous plots. What an unimaginable treat! I thought they were ancient, of course. Now I realize that in the 1950s, the years I was in school and living at home, they were not much older than I am now. But age did not wither their attempts to find men. By the time I got married they were in their seventies and my grandmother's third husband had died. The sisters arrived for the wedding festivities and immediately accosted my twenty-three-year-old groom. "We hear you have two widowed grandfathers," my aunt Eustatia queried. "Why, yes," Steven somewhat bemusedly confirmed. "Is either of them creaky?" came the next question. Steven allowed as how one was creakier than the other. "Well, Co has first pick," said Eustatia to my now astonished about-to-be mate. "After all, her granddaughter found you and they are your grandfathers. I never cut in on Co's men." Neither my grandmother, Corinne, nor my aunt Eustatia walked away with a new groom from my wedding, much to their dismay.

Among the four of them, though they had nine husbands, they only had two children — my mother and my cousin Dinky, my godmother. So Dinky's kids, who were all younger than we were, and Barbara and Tommy and I were the community grandchildren. They took us to movies our parents would have never allowed, drove us down Bourbon Street to see their sister Frosty who lived there, and let us peek in the doors of the strip joints on the way. (When my kids were small, my mother moved into that Bourbon Street house and I used to jokingly chant, "Over the hills and through the woods to grandmother's house we go," as we tripped our way past the denizens of that naughty neighborhood.) When the ladies were middle-aged, it was a great boon to be their only family. Then Dinky died very young. And it was hard on my mother to be the only child of four sisters as they grew old and died. By then, my generation was off starting families of our own.

My great-grandmother enjoyed the whole commotion of her daughter's household immensely, though she didn't participate in the vamping schemes. Instead, she took her pleasures in card games and at the racetrack. I remember once when she was in her nineties, my sister dragged a date to visit "Rets" in the hospital where she was fighting pneumonia. "Poor dear," sympathized the young man, whoever he was, "it's so easy to get sick at her age." "You'd have pneumonia too," Barbara shot back, "if you had spent all day at the races in the rain." When they got to the hospital all my great-grandmother could talk about was the fact that one of her daughters had won the daily double.

When she was about fifteen years old and dating my brother, my sister-in-law, Barbara (yes, it's confusing, two Barbaras, my sister and sister-in-law, but you must admit the rest of the names are interesting), went dutifully to visit Rets, who had the flu. She crept into the room, where the little old lady was sitting up in bed covered by a crocheted afghan. How sweet, Barbara thought, she must be reading the Bible. On closer look she saw the title, *Return to Peyton Place.* Years later, Barbara's daughter, Elizabeth, who had only seen her great-great-grandmother in bed, asked, "Does Rets have legs?"

My children haven't been blessed with the

same sorts of characters entertaining them along the road to adulthood, but they have had a devoted group of family members and friends who have taken a keen interest in them, and for whom they will someday share responsibility. My daughter, Rebecca, already learned that the hard way when she went to Princeton University, partly to be near her aunt Barbara, the closest any of our generation came to genuine "character" status. As the mother of three boys, my sister lusted after a daughter, and readily adopted Becca as her own. The night before school started we were staying at Barbara's house getting ready for a farewell-to-our-daughter dinner. Becca discovered a run in her stockings and went knocking on her aunt's bedroom door, asking to borrow a pair. "I've been waiting all my life for this moment," Barbara announced with much fanfare.

The two of them had a great time together Becca's freshman year. Barbara was running for governor and Becca, who at the age of nine had worked in one of my mother's congressional races, campaigned across the state. She and her aunt were a formidable duo, as Barbara called on Becca to make speeches, or shake hundreds of hands. When our parents moved into a smaller house in New Orleans, they sent the dining room table to Princeton, so it was back in use as campaign central. It was a disappointment, but not a surprise, when Barbara lost the primary, and sophomore year looked like it would be a more leisurely time for aunt and niece to just kick back and enjoy spare moments together. But in October Barbara was diagnosed with incurable cancer, and Becca found herself in a different role. At first it was diversion that was necessary, then errand running and filling in at public events, then helping put together a book of Barbara's poems for publication. ("Becca, I wrote a poem about Christmas. I think I wrote it on a grocery bag and filed it at the mayor's office. It's not in the front of the office, it's in the back, where I keep the borough budget.") Then it was caretaking.

When she went to England over the summer before her junior year, my daughter did so with much trepidation about her aunt. But Barbara's boys were home and needed their own time with their mother. As Becca's junior year began, my sister's condition worsened considerably and her niece became her primary nurse. Barbara felt safe with Becca, secure in her niece's arms when she needed help to the bathroom, unembarrassed in a way she was not even with her husband. While it was not the way most juniors in college spend their time, it was something Becca wouldn't trade for anything. At Barbara's request, Becca sang at her funeral, and I joined her in harmony. And then, after the funeral, after the hundreds of mourners had gone back to their lives, it was Becca who was left in Princeton, bereft of her aunt but still liable for her legacy. So she would go to the various banquets and benefits, accepting awards in Barbara's name, extolling her aunt's virtues, along with those of whatever group sought recognition.

As we grow older, I already see the next generation taking on some of the blessings and burdens of the community of aunts. My niece, Elizabeth, despite the rigors of raising three children while holding down a demanding full-time job, shows up unbidden when anyone is in need. She helped in the arduous task of cleaning out my mother's Washington apartment when she sold it. And my daughter delightedly plays the role of tante to all of the little kids.

Her twin cousins visited her when she lived in Philadelphia. All of the little girl relatives were flower girls at her wedding. What joy these relationships provide! Most of us know how important friends and family are, but it always comes home to us with force at times of great upheaval — births, deaths, moves, marriages. Last year, as both of my children got married, they found themselves surrounded by circles of caring aunts and tantes. Almost all of their "real" aunts and uncles gave parties, welcoming the new young people into the family, and introducing them to their friends. The cousins who had lived six blocks away in New Orleans when I was a little girl, both now live near us in suburban Washington. As they helped with houseguests and homecomings and provided endless hospitality, they also handed on the stories. Our childhood suddenly came alive again, just at the moment I was feeling like an over-the-hill mother of bride and groom.

And my friends — women I'd known over the years as a young wife and then mother, and friends from work who helped me through the growing-up years, trying to mute their giggles during the after-school phone calls ("Rebecca, you have an obligation to go to your piano lesson, you've made a commitment"; "Lee, stop picking on your sister") — all pitched in to make it perfect for my kids. Becca asked my friend Millie, a tante to her, to act in the role of rabbi. She wanted Judaism in the ceremony, but Judaism in a skirt. As I looked at the people gathered together at the weddings, including the people who would now be their families and their warm and welcoming friends, it struck me so strongly that this is what community is all about. A marriage is a formal entrance into the grown-up world, and these would be the people on hand to help in all the transitions involved. The women, especially, will be there in the way they always have been. And then the "kids" will be there for them.

SOLDIER

On the wall above my desk at work is a facsimile copy of the discharge of one "Frank Deming" from the United States Army during the Civil War. Reason for dismissal: "Because of her sex . . . being a female." That's the kind of wonderful present women I've never met send me when we've just debated something on television about women in the military. Recently, we seem to have had a lot of those debates. Revelations about sexual assaults on women in training and the case of a female Air Force pilot's indiscretions with a married man have reinvigorated arguments about women in uniform. The discharge paper of "Frank Deming" is a perceptive viewer's way of informing me that this is not even a slightly new discussion.

It certainly came home to us as a nation that women were playing a significant part in the all-volunteer force during the Persian Gulf War as we watched moms in fatigues kissing their infants farewell. I must admit to some degree of discomfort looking at those pictures, but it was unquestionable that the technology of war had changed so dramatically that brains mattered as much as brawn. And the scenes of those apparently fearless females forced the Pentagon to take another look at the question of women in combat. But, despite the military women's claims that they will never achieve equal status if combat roles are denied them, and despite the protests of those who have been there that they are already exposed to the full dangers of warfare, the politicians persist in fretting over this issue. Out of the forty thousand women who served in the combat area in the Gulf, eleven were killed, two taken prisoner. Still, the brass insists that the public's not ready to accept the concept of women in body bags; also, women cannot be trusted to perform well in combat, and fighting men might make poor judgments in order to protect a romantic interest in the next foxhole. Women in the military tend to give rude responses to those arguments, and their degree of exasperation is understandable — if impolitic — since they have both their own experience and that of women in all of America's wars on their side.

Like so many other areas of female endeavor in the last thirty years, we tend to think that the idea of women on the battlefield is something brand-new under the sun.

It's true that the congressional debate on the Persian Gulf War marked the first time I can remember the phrase "our men and women in the military" used regularly to describe the fighting force. (As a reporter covering the debate, I was struck by this interesting bit of rhetoric and then I realized that it was also the first time I had regularly heard the term "our men in the military." It had always been "our boys in Vietnam" or "our boys in Korea," leading me to the quite delightful observation that this was not the first time a woman had turned a boy into a man.)

There is now in Washington, in addition to the Vietnam women's memorial, an official monument to the women who served in every American conflict. But most people don't seem quite clear on what it is those women did. There was even a commentary on NPR that such a memorial is undeserved because it equates the lowly jobs of women during war with the heroic deeds of men. A little ignorance goes a long way. Even the most cursory of reading reveals that women have been there since the Revolution, carrying the standards into battle, taking up the weapons of those who had fallen, braving the bullets to care for the wounded and dying, brazenly crossing enemy lines as couriers and scouts, daringly tricking ciphers and codes out of Redcoat and Rebel, Vichy leader and Vietcong.

Now that the National Park Service provides reenactments at some battlefield sites, more of us have become aware of the camp followers — the women who went to war with their husbands and sweethearts, doing the cooking and laundry. Many of them also joined the fray. Two well-known figures from the Revolutionary War, Mary Hays, known as Molly Pitcher, and Margaret Corbin, both took their husbands' places on the fields of battle, one at Monmouth, one at Fort Washington. Their heroic exploits have come down to us over the centuries through song and story — Molly "Pitcher" got her nickname because she is supposed to have supplied water to thirsty soldiers — but verification comes through the much more mundane method of researching pension records and teaming that they received military retirement benefits. (Ironically, Revolutionary War pensions were hard to come by for both men and women since the young Republic was financially strapped. Martha Washington had spent so much time as a camp follower herself that she made a cause of the veterans, which was considered a highly political act. So much for the idea that First Ladies sat pouring tea until the modern era.)

Another pensioner whose tales of derring-do are documented was Deborah Samson, who disguised herself as a man, fought through war though twice wounded, and was only found out when she went to the hospital with "brain fever." After the Revolution she made a living entertaining crowds with her stirring speeches: "I threw off the soft habiliment of my sex, and assumed those of the warrior, already prepared for battle." You have the feeling life never was as exciting again.

Then there were the spies. Spying seems to have taken on the status of women's work throughout the country's conflicts. Several from Revolutionary times — women with the sturdy names of Sybil Ludington, Deborah Champion, Lydia Barrington Darragh, Emily Geiger, and Susanna Bolling — risked their lives riding horses over many miles for several days, crossing rivers in the night, sneaking through enemy territory, swallowing rather than surrendering messages, all getting word to the American troops of British plans of attack.

We all know of Dolly Madison's courage in the face of British marauders in the War of 1812, how she saved vital government documents and the portrait of George Washington before escaping from the White

House, where the soldiers added insult to injury by first sitting down to the meal she had prepared before setting fire to the city. We've also read of the famous battles of the U.S.S. *Constitution* (*Old Ironsides*), but most of us didn't know that one of the sailors aboard, George Baker, was actually a woman named Lucy Brewer who lived to tell of her adventures. The battle that gave victory to the United States in that war, a battle fought after the treaty was negotiated, was in my hometown of New Orleans where we grew up hearing of the courage of the Ursuline nuns who collaborated with the American troops.

But it was in the Civil War that the necessity for women became clear. My friend Frank Deming seems to be just one of a great many women who disguised themselves as men in order to fight. One, Jennie Hodgers, was only discovered when she moved into an old soldiers' home at the end of her life; another, a sergeant in General Rosecrans's ranks, had to give up the disguise when she gave birth to a baby. Other women went to war as the equivalent of mascots of regiments, pulling duty as pickets, scouts, and raiders. Several won decorations for their service, others received commissions in the regular army. And again, there was the full complement of spies. Among the best known was Harriet Tubman, who led a union colonel and several hundred black soldiers on a raid that freed eight hundred slaves. For her scouting and spying she was honored with a military funeral at the end of her long life. Then there was the Confederate Belle Boyd, who at the age of seventeen shot and killed a northern soldier for insulting her mother. She then went on to a colorful career as courier and spy which earned her a commission as captain by Stonewall Jackson, and eventual banishment to Canada by the Union. Some women were less lucky — they landed in prison and were even executed for their devotion to duty as they saw it. They must have been doing something of great importance; otherwise, it wouldn't have merited the death penalty.

It was in far more "womanly" tasks, however, that the distaff side distinguished itself in the Civil War. Individual women like "Mother Bickerdyke" went foraging through the fields collecting linens and bandages and boiling them up in giant cauldrons until she was able to get military laundries going. And Annie Wittenmeyer, appalled at the military diet, stared down generals in order to establish wholesome kitchens in the hospitals.

When these women faced opposition from the military leaders they threatened to go to the press to expose the conditions of the fighting forces. But early in the war, it became clear that more than individual efforts were needed, that neither the Confederate nor Union governments was equipped to deal with huge numbers of soldiers going off to war. There was no Red Cross (something that was later remedied by another Civil War heroine, Clara Barton), no USO, no organization to feed, clothe, or nurse the vast armies called into service. Chaos ensued as families tried to get provisions willy-nilly to soldiers at the front. So Louisa Schuyler, a great-granddaughter of Alexander Hamilton, convened a mass meeting at Cooper Union in New York to organize for soldiers' relief. Out of that grew the U.S. Sanitary Commission, largely staffed by women volunteers who managed to supply the troops from community warehouses, which they established all over the country. To raise money for their wares, women staged elaborate "sanitary fairs" in major cities where they auctioned off such items as the original Emancipation Proclamation. Over the course of the war the fairs brought in more than twenty-five million dollars.

One of the things that interested me most

as I learned this history was how reluctant the commanders were to accept women as nurses. It came as a surprise to me that there had been no system for caring for the wounded before the Civil War. Apparently, fellow soldiers and camp followers had always done the nursing in the past. But as women saw the great need for their services to treat the ever-growing numbers of bodies filled with sickness and shrapnel, they started working, unbidden, in the hospitals. At first this caused great consternation, and the Confederate Congress ordered an investigation of the hospitals to see if women were doing any harm. The report revealed that the mortality rate in female-run hospitals was half that of those run by men. The Congress then passed laws giving women control of the hospitals, and gave "preference in all cases to females" in lower-level jobs, causing much grumbling by the men about "petticoat government."

In the north, Dorothea Dix, a well-known crusader for the rights of the mentally ill, went to the acting surgeon general soon after the war began to propose that she recruit a nursing corps of women volunteers. To answer the doctors' concerns that bringing women into the hospitals would cause sexual scandal, Dix agreed that "No woman under thirty years need apply to serve in government hospitals," and "All nurses are required to be very plain-looking women. Their dresses must be brown or black, with no bows, no curls, no jewelry and no hoop-skirts." In addition, they were required to bring letters of recommendation from their pastors! The history books tell us that no scandals ensued but a few nurses were transferred because of "impertinence" to surgeons.

It was in this role as nurses that the military began eventually to admit women officially into the ranks. Female nurses were recruited for the Spanish-American War at the end of the nineteenth century, then established in law at the beginning of the twentieth, first the Army Nurse Corps in 1901, then the Navy Nurse Corps in 1908. In all, about twenty thousand of these women served in World War I, when the Navy also established the "Yeomanettes" and the Marines the "Marinettes," mostly for clerical work. After the war the services demobilized the almost thirteen thousand women enlistees.

By the time World War II was declared the women were ready. The Women's Voluntary Services started training ambulance drivers, first-aid workers, and mobile kitchen forces more than a year before Pearl Harbor. Congresswoman Edith Nourse Rogers steered through legislation establishing the Women's Army Auxiliary Corps, which allowed women to serve but gave them no military status and no benefits. That changed in 1943, when the "Auxiliary" was dropped and the WACs became official members of the armed forces. The Navy equivalent — the WAVES (Women Accepted for Volunteer Emergency Service) — had been created by Congress a year earlier. In the course of the war one hundred forty thousand women served in the Army, one hundred thousand in the Navy, and another one hundred thousand went as Coast Guard personnel and Red Cross nurses. The need for nurses was such that Congresswoman Frances Bolton successfully passed into law creation of the Cadet Nurse Corps, where those who promised to serve the government's military or civilian needs were provided federal funds for nursing school. Still, the constant call for nurses was such that President Roosevelt asked Congress to draft nurses into the military. The measure passed the House and was still before the Senate when the war ended. And to think that much of the argument about women in the military and the ill-fated Equal Rights

Amendment concerned what was considered the big taboo of drafting women! Not surprisingly, when the demand was great, the debate was not.

I remember as a little girl wanting to be a WAVE, and trying to devise a Navy uniform out of my wardrobe. It was a time when everyone's house had pictures of all the men in the family in uniform. My father had been in the Navy for the war, so of course, that was the branch I chose. As it turned out, I later went to Wellesley College, where former president Mildred McAfee Horton had been the first captain in charge of the WAVES. Colonel Oveta Culp Hobby, who commanded the WACs, was a prominent figure in 1950s Washington as a member of President Eisenhower's cabinet. Though I never met them, these were women of great stature in my girlhood, women to be admired and emulated.

There were also the Women's Air Force Service Pilots (or WASPS), who flew right into the action but were never accorded full military status. In a book of letters from women in the military in World War II, *We're in This War, Too*, the excitement of pilot Marion Stegeman of Athens, Georgia, sounds like any flyboy you've ever talked to. "Mother," she wrote from her training in

Texas in 1943, "you haven't lived until you get way up there — all alone — just you and that big, beautiful plane humming under your control." When it became clear that the Army Air Forces had a glut of pilots and the WASPS weren't going to get the status they expected, Marion consulted her mother about whether she should resign and get married instead. "How about a long letter of advice from you — and also please ask Aunt Helvig and Grannie what they think." It might be a new set of questions for the women of the family, but she trusted their judgment. When it became clear that the WASPS would not be recognized, Marion Stegeman, understanding that she would be in a precarious position in the future, quit. But many other women continued to serve, and risked enormous dangers. They finally achieved the praise and pensions they deserved in 1977 when my own mother spearheaded the effort in Congress to pay these pilots their due. (She tells a funny story about getting cosponsors for the bill to support the WASPS. One old-line Protestant male colleague said as he signed, "I don't know what your bill does, but there are so few of us WASPS left, could I sign on to it too?")

Marion Stegeman went home, but most

of the other letters are from women who fought through the war, and they are some of the most affecting you would ever want to read. These women are so incredibly competent and unfailingly compassionate that I find my eyes filling with tears as I peer into their pasts. It also makes me angry that anyone would claim that they were in anything but the most essential and exposed positions. Here's a nurse writing her parents from Pearl Harbor: "The wounded started coming in 10 minutes after the first attack. . . . Then comes the second attack — We all fell face down on the wounded in the halls, O.R. and everywhere and heard the bombers directly over us. We had no helmets nor gas masks. . . . One of the soldiers who works for my ward saw me and so we shared helmets together. In the meantime the bombs were dropping all around us and when a 500 lb. bomb dropped about [censored] from the [censored] . . . then they were gone." And that, it goes without saying, was just the beginning.

Women in combat fatigues waded ashore in the North African invasion in 1942, arrived in Normandy on D-Day plus four in June 1944, and by July were in France in force. The stories of Red Cross workers landing in war zones and somehow setting up cheery cafés complete with curtains and coffee along with their trademark doughnuts never cease to amaze me. And then there are the agonizing letters from Anzio. "There is nothing to write about but the wounded," June Wandrey confided in her parents in June 1944. "We live down in the ground in sand-bagged, damp, smelly foxholes." Foxholes where they not only worked to make their patients whole but constantly battled to save them, and themselves, from strafing.

There were flight nurses in the Pacific who would toil through the night keeping their charges alive in body and soul, and then rush to put on makeup before landing to fulfill regulations that nurses look attractive and fresh as hospital vessels hit ground, regulations these women write about very matter-of-factly. They were women fighting constantly for normalcy in an insane world. There's the wonderfully refreshing letter of Billie Oliver from New Guinea a couple of weeks before her marriage, asking her parents, "Will you please get me a real sexy nightgown. You know, the kind a bride would wear. . . . After all, I will have to get married in uniform. I'd like to let my boy know he's got a woman, not a soldier."

He had, of course, a woman and a soldier. That's something these women learned about themselves. Army nurse Helen McKee wrote her parents from Italy right after VE Day about one boy for whom the war lasted just a few days too long — he had lost his arm and both eyes: "Of course, we are supposed to be accustomed to seeing handless arms, and your ears should be deaf to the groans of agony from these poor souls, but alas the two years of combat has not hardened the heart. . . . I don't think anyone felt closer, or shared the pain of these boys more than we, the A.N.C. Now we have finished our jobs, we've seen the war thru. We are tired and ready to come home." But for some there was still more to come. June Wandrey had left Italy and gone on to Germany. There, after the war in Europe was officially over, she found herself treating the victims of Dachau. "I'm on night duty with one hundred corpse-like patients," she wrote her parents in a horrifyingly vivid account. "God, where are you?"

It was a question asked in war in every century. And it was a question especially asked by women, who since the time of Lysistrata have been on record as ardent enemies of armed conflict. Public opinion polling from its inception has shown women more opposed to war than men. And yet, ironically, wars have the effect of improving the economic lives of many women. So it was in the Civil War that women went to work in government agencies and arsenals. Southern women became shopkeepers and teachers in numbers that required the upgrading of women's education. And in World War II six million women who had never worked outside the home joined the civilian labor force. African-American women moved from domestic work to factories. Half the rural black female labor force found jobs in the cities. Taking an editorial look at all this change the *Minnesota Tribune* in August 1942 asked the question, "WACs and WAVES and women welders. . . . Where is it all going to end? . . . Is it hard to foresee after the boys come marching home and they marry these emancipated women, who is going to tend the babies in the next generation?" The answer, to no one's real surprise, turned out to be the women. But, despite all efforts to put the genie back in the bottle, the world for women would never be the same again.

The campaign to send Rosie the Riveter home to the split-level ranch house largely succeeded. But women who had performed for this nation both overseas and on the home front knew what they had done and were proud of it. That generation of women raised the huge postwar baby boom and created all this modern confusion about a woman's place. After the war, there never seemed to be a right answer. But one place that had forever changed was the military, where women had come into their own and would insist on staying.

FIRST-CLASS
MECHANIC

"I'm a mechanic, first class." I wish I could adequately describe the breadth and brightness of the smile on Eva Oliver's face as she said those words. They represented the fulfillment of an incredible struggle up out of welfare and into the successful pursuit of the American dream.

This conversation with Eva Oliver took place in the cheery house she built with her own hands on an acre of land just outside Baton Rouge, Louisiana. I first met her in Washington where she had traveled to receive an award from the National Commission on Working Women, and when I heard the outlines of her story I knew that I wanted to learn more about her. My chance came when the producers of *This Week with David Brinkley* told the program's participants that, for the second year in a row, we could each interview anyone we wanted for the Christmas broadcast. What an opportunity! On a television show watched religiously by Washington policymakers, I could actually talk at some length to someone their decisions directly affected.

The bare facts were these — at the age of thirty, with two tiny children, Eva Oliver, welfare recipient, enrolled in a state-sponsored training program that placed her in a job at Allied Signal, a huge chemical company in Baton Rouge. She had moved up in the job to the position of first-class mechanic, the first African-American woman to achieve that position. One of her children was in college, another ready to join the military to pay for her college education. Ms. Oliver had moved out of her dangerous city neighborhood to an area of fenced-in yards, friendly neighbors, and fine vegetable gardens. She had built her own house in the evenings and on weekends when she wasn't performing a backbreaking job at Allied. In her spare time she counseled women on welfare.

The bare facts were impressive enough, but I knew the full story of this tough, capable lady had to be truly interesting. So the camera crew and I arrived on Eva Oliver's doorstep a little before Christmas Day 1994. And we listened to Mrs. Oliver, a tall, open-faced woman, ready with a big laugh or a big hug, tell her tale.

"I did the welfare thing, I drew unemployment, I did a day's work anywhere I could get a day's work because I had to survive. Then you turn around and you make mistakes in your life and you get to where you made so many that they all stack up. And life is about making choices. That's number one. Please, God, make good choices in your life. And if you make the bad choices and you get down to the bottom, then you have to do something about it."

The something that Eva Oliver did was listen to a minister who kept coming around asking her what she was doing, and kept urging her to go to the state office of women's services. She'd agree but never follow through. Finally, the minister gave her a name and number of someone there, and Ms. Oliver called and explained that she wanted to work in a plant, where she knew the pay was good, but she had no training whatsoever. The state agent gave her the information that they were starting a training program for blue-collar women and Eva Oliver applied for the class. She was rejected. Despite the discouragement she had the guts to press on. "I went down to see them and I told her, 'I'm not going to take no for an answer.' So they sent the head of the program down and I told him, 'This is no joke for me. I have two kids. I can't get a job, I need some training. I don't know what else to do, can you-all please help me?' And he said, 'Because of your determination, if anybody fails the physical, I'll let you know.' " Two days later he called and said, "You're in."

It was a training program that paid students the minimum wage while they were in school. That combined with her mother and sisters' willingness to care for the kids made it possible for Eva Oliver to get the skills she needed, and she went from being the last person accepted into the class to the first one hired out of it. Getting the job turned out to be the easy part. The hard part was doing it. She remembers with a laugh how terrified she was standing over a bubbling acid pit in nearly one-hundred-degree heat, digging holes. "I took this little shovel and I stood out there and I dug and I dug and I dug. And I prayed the whole time. I said, 'Oh God, please, Jesus. Let me handle this. I got insurance on my kids and I'm going to be able to take care of myself. I can't lose this, please, Lord, help me.' And I dug those six holes. It took me a week to do it, but I dug those six holes. And at the end I said, 'Why, thank you, God.' And I think I realized that you can do anything you put your mind to. And that worked out, because after I got my first paycheck I said, 'I don't care where it's at, I'll be there.' "

Listening to Eva Oliver talk about what a "scary experience" it was for her to go for the first time into a plant, I could almost feel along with her the sense of being overwhelmed by pipes and wires, almost smell the acid pit as she described it. It made me a little suspicious about what was going on there. Were they testing her, seeing if the woman was up to the job? "I think they wanted to know right off hand does she want to turn and run at the first hard thing that comes along. I think they wanted to know right off hand would she stand it." And, she added, the men worried about their own security, did women coming into the plant mean women would take their jobs? But they eventually became friends and the men accepted the women, with what she calls just a little hassling here and there. "Sometimes emotion with women will come up. And you ran to the bathroom and you do your little crying and then you wipe your eyes and come back out. But it was hard. And for me it wasn't a choice."

That's the theme Eva Oliver struck over and over again. For her it wasn't a choice. She had to do this work. It was her way out, her salvation. From what? From welfare. "Collecting a check from the state is a trap as far as I see it. I wanted better. I didn't want to be dependent on anybody. I didn't want anybody to tell me how I can live or what I can do. And it's something that makes you lie. If you get a day's work and you make fifty dollars, you're not going to turn that day's work in. But it's a trap because when the youngest child turns eighteen, you don't have any retirement. You don't have any Social Security. You don't have anything. You're just an old person who raised all your kids on welfare."

This wise woman made so much sense. Here's her explanation of how crime got started among kids whose mothers are on welfare: "What you could buy for a two-year-old, you can't buy for a fifteen-year-old. So now, you're really in trouble because you've got a fifteen-year-old kid and you're still getting the same money that you started getting five years ago. So then, that's when you've got the tennis shoes that you can't afford and your kid wants to be like everybody and you can't afford to give it to him. And then he ends up on the streets." She talked about how "project women" raised "project kids." "Once you learn how to deal with the system, that little two-year-old or that little three-year-old is sitting there looking at you maneuver. And then she learns how to maneuver. And then it repeats itself over and over and over again. And I didn't want that for my children. My mother didn't give it to me, and I didn't want that for my children."

Eva Oliver knew she wanted out of "the system." As she says, that check that comes for free comes with too high a price. But she doesn't think that women on welfare can simply pull themselves up by the bootstraps, go out and find jobs and become constructive members of society. It's not that simple. And as she concocted her prescription for the welfare mess, I wished I could pack her onto the plane with me, bring her back to Washington to talk to people writing the laws.

"I think the answer is it's better to help a person some and let him help himself some. And then, as he helps himself, then give him less until it balances out. In other words it's like raising a child. Once you have it, you have to keep nurturing it until it grows to stand on its two feet. So, just saying, 'In two years we're going to cut them off' — no. Because you created this system and kept them babies all this time. And now, all of a sudden, you're going to cut the cord? Uh-uh. That won't work."

What does work, according to Eva Oliver,

is a good training program. Those programs have come in for a lot of criticism as an ineffective and costly use of taxpayer dollars. She herself had once been in a Job Corps program that didn't make her self-sufficient. What was it about this training that made the difference? "They gave us a lot of love. They made you believe in yourself. It was a hug, a pat on the hand. It was a time of healing. It was a time of learning. They taught you how to dress for an interview, how to talk, what to say, what not to say. And they gave you that extra pat on the back: 'Girl, you can do it. This is the greatest class that ever came through here.' And then they sent you out of the door, and you went out with your little bag swinging in your hand, 'I'm going to conquer the world.' " If the first job didn't come through, they'd send you to another, giving the sense all the time that they cared, that they believed. How simple. And how rare.

But even with that kind of encouragement, Eva Oliver would not have made it, she's convinced, without her family. She had the values of hard work and perseverance passed down by her father and mother and grand-mothers, and she had her sisters and brothers pitching in to take care of her kids when she worked the swing shift, or stayed for overtime. "Everybody's not going to be in the same situation that I was in, that I had sisters and brothers so close around me. But then, you look through the community and you find somebody who can help you with your kids. And if you have to pay them, then pay them. Working gives you your pride and dignity back. And then you, in turn, pass that down to your kids and say, 'If you work hard, you can have all the good things in life, too. You don't have to take the shortcuts like stealing something out of a grocery store. If you work for something you can walk in and demand somebody sell this to you.'"

It's a message she conveys not only to her own children, but to many women on welfare. Eva Oliver believes deeply in "giving back." She's picked up the rent and utility bills of other women in need, she's even taken some into her home. Her phone number, she admits, is "all over the place," as a resource for other women. She also goes to the training center and works with the women coming up through the program. Her company, Allied Signal, gives her time to go proselytize to other welfare mothers about the value of work. But, she warns, don't go for a blue-collar job unless you're ready for it. "Most women will come out and say, 'I don't have to do this.' So they'll walk away from it. If you're sure this is what you want to do, fine. For God's sake, go ahead. But if you're not sure, then don't mess it up for somebody else." It's tough, tough work at Allied Signal, Eva Oliver advises other women, made tougher for her because she didn't start until she was thirty years old. Her age might have made her situation more difficult, but even younger women share her need to compensate for the fact that she doesn't have the same physical strength as a man. "When my muscle wears out, my brain kicks in," she says with a laugh.

And she keeps learning. When I talked to her she was in welding school: "I'll probably forever be in somebody's school doing something. And I think everybody should. If you want to be successful, then educate yourself. This is the key. We just browbeat this: 'You have to go to school, you have to go to school, you have to go to school.' If you work hard in school, then you can have the American dream. You can have the house, the family, the car, or whatever it is that you want to be." It's the oldest of messages from American parents to their children. But somewhere along the way it got lost in the welfare system. The connection somehow got severed. No one believed it was possible, that the old "Go to school, work hard, and you will succeed" adage applied to them. Eva Oliver is doing her best to bring it back, both for her own kids and for dozens of women she counsels and cares for. "It's just like you've got to help. You've got to give something back. I felt like I had gotten so much, and God has left me so much that I had to give something back." She's now "giving back" to one of the sisters who helped her when she was down. With her own kids now working and on their own, Eva Oliver is raising a twelve-year-old niece whose mother has been incapacitated by a stroke.

When I recently checked in with Ms. Oliver she told me that she's now serving on the Governor's Workforce Development Commission, educating the State of Louisiana on welfare-to-work proposals. She admits that it's not getting any easier doing the backbreaking work of a first-class mechanic. And there are times when all she wants in the world is to shed the hard hat and overalls and doll up in earrings and high-heeled shoes. But she's going to keep at it until retirement age because she knows "when you accomplish something it really makes you feel great." Then Eva Oliver thinks she'd like to raise flowers and travel and enjoy life. I wouldn't bet on it.

FRIEND

What would we do without our women friends? I can't imagine how we could survive without the hugs and humor, the closeness and Kleenex that our female friendships provide. Men often envy the importance that friends play in our lives — and they should. It's a special relationship women share that most men seem to have trouble achieving. For all the talk about male bonding, I think a lot of men find friendship with a woman easier than friendship with another man, I know my husband does. Obviously, I'm no expert here and volumes have been written by those who are; all I can talk about with any authority are my own personal experiences.

From the time my father went to Congress, when Barbara and Tommy were babies and I wasn't yet born, our family lived in Washington while Congress was in session, which was from January through summer, and in New Orleans when it was on recess from summertime till January. When Barbara started school, that meant switching in January from one school to another, and that's what we did for many years. We always joked that by the time the teachers caught on to us we were out of there, and our parents finally decided that we would be better educated if we spent the whole school year in one place. So, after my third-grade year we started going to school year-round in Washington. Because I stopped going to school there as such a little kid, I didn't have many friends in New Orleans, unlike my sister and brother. When I arrived there for the summer the other kids were already separated into their little cliques where there wasn't any room for me, and I missed my Washington friends terribly. We would write long letters saying absolutely nothing, pore over them, and eagerly await the next. My cousins, who had no choice in the matter, became my best friends in Louisiana. In the end that's been a boon for me because family ties keep us close, closer than I would be with other childhood friends. And after my sister died it was especially important to me to have the comfort of family members who had shared my childhood.

One cousin, Jo Pepper Morrison, is related to me on both my mother and father's side. (Don't ask.) When we were little kids I would haughtily tell her that she had no relatives who weren't also my relatives, but I had relatives who weren't also hers. Since she is one of seven children, it didn't break her heart to lose out on the extended relative lottery. Jo's mother is my father's sister, and I spent long periods of the summer in the family compound on the Mississippi Gulf Coast where she and my grandparents and other aunts and uncles all lived. After we got tired of the scene there, Jo Pepper and I would board a Trailways bus and travel to Pointe Coupee Parish in Louisiana where my mother's mother, who was also Jo's aunt, would take over. We whiled away part of the long sultry summer on horseback, riding into the tiny town of Lettsworth where there was a general store and a post office, and exploring the various haunts on the farm. (It belonged to my grandmother's second husband's brother-in-law, no relation to us whatsoever, but "Uncle Billy" put up with us year in and year out.) Mostly we read. One summer I read all of *Gone with the Wind* out loud to Jo and quizzed her at the end of each chapter to make sure she was listening. As the youngest child in my family, I was thrilled to have someone younger than me to boss around, even though the difference in our age is only six months. We still laugh a lot about that summer and others where we wondered what all those words meant in the *Reader's Digest* condensed version of *The Grapes of Wrath* and other such steamy (for the 1950s) novels.

My cousins Courtney and Barbara Manard were just on either side of me in age, and lived only six blocks away in New Orleans. We took swimming lessons together at the local park and somehow survived without contracting some dread disease, then we went back to their house where we devised and acted out myriad imaginary tableaux. I'd tag along with them to their grandmother's house, even though she was no relation to me, where we all played a mean game of canasta. Their other grandmother, my great-aunt, lived on a Spanish-moss-draped tree-studded plantation near Baton Rouge. There picking pecans consumed our time — after all we were paid eleven cents a pound. Barbara and Courtney now live near me in suburban Washington, Courtney's daughter Christine is my godchild, and we share the great solace of knowing that we will always be there for each other.

My family moved into the house I still live in when I was eight years old. It's odd in modern America to settle into the family homestead; it's particularly odd in the Washington, D.C., area, where almost everyone hails from someplace else. People often ask me what it's like to cook in my mother's kitchen, to sleep in my parents' bedroom. Actually, it's quite wonderful. In the years after Steve and I were married and moved away, we took a part of home with us. My parents' early nineteenth-century cherry bed had been moved to the attic when they went for a king-size model. Steve and I decided to liberate it, and Mamma drove it in a U-Haul to New York, where we installed it in our first apartment. The bed then moved around the world with us to California and Greece, until it came back to the old bedroom in Bethesda. There it remains.

Living in my mother and father's house has allowed for continuity for the family over the decades, plus continuing friendships. My sister and I went to Stone Ridge, a private Catholic girls' school run by the rigorously intellectual but also deeply fun-loving Religious of the Sacred Heart. The nuns took us seriously as young women, making it clear that we could be anything we wanted to be in this society. (I tease them now that the only role they tacitly closed off to us was that of priest, and they clearly weren't happy about that.) We were part of the group of kids who ran the student government, acted in the plays, organized the events, put out the school newspaper and yearbook. I was the klutzy one, but the others all starred on the athletic teams, which even in that era counted at a girls' school. The daring stuff we did was so square as to be embarrassing — sneaking cigarettes, driving by boyfriends' houses to see if they were home, listening to Johnny Mathis and the Kingston Trio in each other's dens when we should have been studying. Little did we know then that the friendships formed from those silly pastimes, the countless hours on the telephone, the sleepovers where no one slept, would in later years bring us back together through happy times and sad — through marriages and births and deaths, runaway kids and runaway husbands.

Barbara and I were one of three groups of sisters in our respective grades. Until she died my sister stayed close with my friends' older sisters, and they are still part of our family lives. Clare Pratt is now a nun, a Religious of the Sacred Heart living in Rome, where my mother moved last year when she took the job of U.S. Ambassador to the Vatican. Clare keeps an occasional eye on my mother, no easy task, and I keep in touch with her mother here. Her sister Cinda was not only my best friend in high school, we roomed together in college as well. She now lives in the San Francisco Bay Area and checks in on my daughter on occasion. Carol Sweeterman had so much history with our family that she didn't shy away from telling Steve years ago that he wasn't doing the right thing by our son, Lee, who desperately wanted to switch from public to private school. Steven objected for reasons that had little to do with Lee's own needs and wants and Carol had the standing to tell Steve the hurtful truth. Carol's sons are so close to my sister's sons that we can count on them to show up on Christmas night, without fail. Often their cousin Laura, daughter of my old and good friend Anne, drops by as well since she's become my son's friend. In fact, our house seems to attract the children of our old friends, returning like homing pigeons to the place their mothers spent so much of their young lives.

Going to a women's college meant making even more solid friendships that we've easily nurtured over time. Twice in recent years, six of us have even managed to escape to what my son only slightly jokingly calls "sisterhood is powerful" getaways. After the few years at Wellesley where we all lived under the same roof, we spread out over the country, so we have to make a concerted effort to see each other. Since several of our kids are each other's godchildren, we often use them as an excuse. My daughter Becca's wedding brought everyone here last year, but I just got a brief breakfast with my old buddies, since I had to do duty as mother of the bride. Whenever we do reunite we're only sorry that we don't do it more often; it's remarkable how we're able to just pick up where we left off, even though on the face of it we lead wildly different lives.

It's interesting how in each stage of life new female friends emerge, and how they stay friends forever. As a young working girl fresh out of college my friend Eden Lipson, whom I had met through student politics, thankfully came to Washington, which seemed like a real "guy place" at the time. (Maybe it still does, but I'm so used to it, how would I know?) One of the last of my friends to get married — remember this was the mid-sixties when you were deemed an old maid at twenty-two — Eden could be counted on to visit us wherever we moved, and to introduce us to her legions of friends while there. Once in California with my second child about due we were driving across a winding canyon road when I started having contractions. Eden managed to keep me, the big baby, and the car under control until things calmed down. Rebecca didn't come for a few more days, but that experience cemented the friendship across the generations even before birth. Eden published Becca's book reviews in the *New York Times* and gave the first party after she announced her engagement. And Eden's kids are close to me as well. One is my godson.

While I was working in Washington after college, my boss asked if my mother might know someone who could work for just a few days a week, maybe a young mother. My mother instantly came up with the name Jean Firstenberg because Jeannie had helped Mamma with the Johnson inauguration. Even though she's only eight years older than I am, Jeannie became the older woman I could confide in, the way I now am for younger women at work. We'd go to her house after work to sip Dubonnet and plot ways to convince Steve to propose while her kids, Debbie and Doug, then seven and five, vied with me for their mom's attention. Now Debbie works with my son, Lee, in London and Doug is my neighbor and good friend, whose little girl, Lindy, named for my mother, is Steve's and my godchild.

It was hard on me when the Firstenbergs moved to New York, but I soon followed after Steven and I got married. I was glad to have them as friends because most of our friendships were pretty well determined by the *New York Times*, where Steve was a (very) young reporter. We mostly hung out with Timesmen and their wives, and all the talk was of the *Times* — the overheated institutional gossip seemed our only common currency. That might have been true for the men, most of whom have not stayed in close touch. For the women, though we participated in the conversation and enjoyed the juicy tidbits at least as much as the guys, it turned out something deeper and much longer lasting was also being said — "I am your friend, I understand you, you can count on me." More than thirty years later most of the men are no longer at the *Times* and several of the couples are no longer married, but the women still matter a great deal to one another. When Rebecca got married, some of those old friends gave her a shower. When it came time to write this book, I turned for help with the research to one of them, Anne Charnley, who had been a guest at my very first dinner party.

Intensity, I think, characterizes the friendships you make when your children are small. The hours spent together huddled in chilly playgrounds, held hostage in fast-food restaurants, or holding each other's tear-streaked toddlers creates an intimacy that isn't always there in later life. In my case in those years, particularly strong friendships were forged by tragedy. We had moved to California and made some casual acquaintances, and an old friend from school worked with me on a TV show, but there wasn't that instant circle of colleagues that the *Times* provided in New York. Steve was one of only a few people in the Los Angeles Bureau and he was on the road much of the time. Then some Washington friends asked friends of theirs in California to look us up and they kindly did. At their house I met Millie Harmon, and we hit it off instantly, so we started a weekly playgroup with another friend of hers. While Steve and I were visiting our parents over the summer, Millie's twenty-nine-year-old husband was killed in a rafting accident. She had three little children, no sisters and brothers, her husband had no sisters or brothers, his parents were dead, and her father was dead. It was clear that her friends would be her family. And so we were.

We spent many waking hours together. We granted her crying rights for herself, and bragging rights for her children. We spent all significant days and holidays as a newly crafted family. When not quite a year had passed since Ellis had been killed, Millie said, "I'd like to do one of these holidays myself, I think I'm ready." She decided that an Easter brunch would work for her and I was relieved since I was cooking the annual Passover seder and it was going to be a lot of entertaining in just a few days' time. So we agreed on a plan. Millie said, "Then it's set, you do Passover, I'll do Easter." Then we burst out laughing — she's Jewish, you see, and I'm Catholic. But that's the way it was for many years and still Millie almost always makes it to Passover at our house.

When a few years later the airplane my father was traveling in disappeared, it was Millie's turn to console and comfort me. While I was in Alaska for the early days of the search, Lee turned four. We had a birthday party scheduled at Disneyland the next weekend. Millie got the cake and organized the kids so that when I returned all I had to do was try to cope with Winnie the Pooh for President while reeling from the still unsolved mystery of my father's disappearance.

After we moved to Greece, Millie met a terrific guy and they eventually got married. It was a treat when they moved to New York after we had moved back to Washington — no longer did a continent divide us. The other close couple from those terrible but tender days in California, Meredith and Tom Brokaw, had also migrated to New York, so happy days were here again. Then, shockingly, incredibly, Millie's second husband was killed in a car crash. And the circle of friends closed around her again. It seemed only a few years before that I had spoken at their wedding; now I was speaking at his funeral.

As exciting and interesting as it was, going to Greece to live meant leaving thirty years of friends behind. Fortunately, our kids were three and five, so my first task was finding schools for them. With school comes community, and with community comes friendship. I've often said that I would never move again without school-aged children — they force you out of any innate shyness. A couple of my good friends from the time in Greece now live in the United States and we've kept in touch over the years, visiting each other in good times, reaching out to each other in bad. While we were abroad lots of friends came to visit, and friends would give their friends who were traveling to the Aegean our phone number. Eden told her buddies Aaron Latham and Lesley Stahl to give us a call. We had never met them, but were delighted to invite them over. Lesley still talks about that day, watching me carry Becca, who was so big her body practically covered mine, seeing what a kick we got from our kids. She and Aaron decided on the spot that a child was a good idea, and proceeded to produce one. I've always teased Taylor Latham that she should be grateful that Lee and Becca were behaving well that day. I knew instantly that Lesley and I would be fast friends if we ever ended up in the same city at the same time.

That opportunity came when we moved back to Washington and I learned the unmatchable value of female friends in the workplace. I was pretty depressed about the move. That's an understatement — I was a first-class witch about it. I felt like I had just gotten my sea legs as a reporter, successfully free-lancing for CBS News and several magazines, that my kids were a good age to stay abroad, and that Steve's folks and my mother were still young and healthy enough that they didn't need us back in the United States. I really wanted to see more of the world through another foreign posting, but I was counting on Steve to do that for me — I had no offers of my own, and as far as I was concerned at the time, no opportunities of my own. But the *New York Times* had other plans, and Steven was ready to return to Washington, so I had no choice but to come along, kicking and screaming the whole way. (Well, I could have come along nicely, but what fun would that have been?) We waited to move until the school year was about to begin, so the kids wouldn't be hanging around bored and friendless. Then we barged in on Mamma, who moved into my old room with Rebecca and gave Steven and me the master bedroom. There was a flurry of shopping for school clothes for the kids and work clothes for Steve, as it had been a while since he had been on a beat where a suit was required. Then the day came when I waved them all off in their new outfits to their new lives and went back inside my old home and burst into tears. What now for me? The prospect of pounding the pavement for a job — something I had done over and over as we moved around the country and the world — that prospect was so disheartening I could hardly stand it. Although I had already had a couple of preliminary interviews, I knew it wasn't going to be easy.

When Steven got to work he found himself seated next to a woman he didn't know. She told him that she had just been hired and had been working at National Public Radio. "Does that mean your job there's now open?" my always-on-the-alert husband asked. "Yes," she answered, "why?" "Because I have a wife looking for a job." "Call Nina Totenberg" came the response. He called and Nina said, "Get her résumé right over here." He did, and the rest, as they say, is history. In any event, that's the way Steven tells the story.

The rest, actually, was a good bit harder than that. But it was made considerably easier, as my life has been made easier in the more than twenty years since, by the fact that Nina Totenberg and Linda Wertheimer were at NPR, urging me on, and egging on the bosses to hire me. Linda had graduated from Wellesley the year after me, and though we didn't know each other there, the alma mater tie existed. It was the first time in my more than a dozen years in the work force that anything resembling an old girls' network rose up to envelop me. Nina and Linda helped me learn the things I didn't know, forced the guys to acknowledge the things I did know, and supported me through the treacherous first few months when the bosses couldn't decide whether to hire me or not, even though they were putting my stories on the air every day. Finally the three of us succeeded in getting me the job — believe me, it would not have happened had I just been on my own.

We were in our early thirties then; in the

years since we have had the kind of working relationship and familial relationship that's rare at best, impossible more often. On the job, we've filled in for each other both by showing up someplace where the other one can't be, or by filling in facts in a story, doing some extra reporting that gives it extra heft, or listening to something sensitive to make sure we're not courting trouble. We've also helped fight each other's battles so consistently that a boss knows he's likely to be taking on all three of us if he takes on one of us. For years we sat together in the newsroom, where both our high-volume laughter and our low-pitched whispers seemed to intimidate the men, much to our delight. One horrified colleague called our little corner "The Fallopian Jungle." In truth what we were doing was sharing — sharing joys, hopes, fears, and sorrows. We had at last in the world of work found women like ourselves. We had suffered discrimination and harassment at a time when that just simply was the way it was and now we were in positions of some influence in our organization where we could help each other and the younger women coming along after us.

But our friendship far transcends the shared stories of the workplace. Lots has happened to us in these twenty-plus years.

Nina got married, and Linda and I were her ushers. Linda's mother died and my sister died and we kept each other together through those times. When Barbara was sick, Linda and Nina spelled each other on vacation so that I wouldn't be alone. When she died, Linda and her husband, Fred, came rushing home from vacation to be with me. My friends held me, shaking and sobbing, knowing the depths of what I felt, and knowing they would have to get me through the next few painful months.

Right before her fiftieth birthday, Nina's husband took a fall on the ice that caused his brain to hemorrhage. He spent months in intensive care, then in a regular hospital room, then in rehabilitation. Linda and I were there with Nina, sitting through lectures from the neurosurgeon, using our reporting skills first to understand the workings of the brain, and then the workings of the health care system. Floyd finally went home and was well on his way to mending when a routine checkup showed a spot on his lungs. There followed another several months of near-fatal experiences after lung surgery. Nina and Floyd were both incredibly valiant through all of this, but Nina would be the first to say that she could not have done it without her friends keeping vigil with her. We were there for her always, in the way we know she'll always be there for us.

Though we three have a particularly close relationship, the support system of women working in Washington is wonderfully strong. For years we had a fabulously frivolous ladies' lunch where we traded tales of the people in our trades, and tips on the problems of our age. Hot gossip and hot flashes shared equal billing. But there were times when other purposes took precedence. At one lunch a member of our group walked in looking stricken. She had just been fired that morning. Lesley Stahl got right on the phone and by the end of the day, our friend had a job. It was a moment we'll always remember because it showed that finally we could do what the guys had always been able to do — that we had the power to come through for our friends beyond offering a shoulder to cry on. These ritual meals women take together provide food for the soul. The nine women in the Senate hold regular dinner meetings, which make their male colleagues hilariously nervous, but give the women a brief respite from the pomposity and preening. Our ladies' lunch fell on hard times after Lesley Stahl moved away. She's such a good friend that she's willing to do the organizing, so now we lazily count on her to visit Washington to get us all together again.

Now that we're among the older women in the workplace, we find we can make a difference for the younger women both personally and professionally, and that's very satisfying. Linda and Nina and I are such meddlers that we often try to arrange love lives as well as advise on work lives. Our greatest triumph along these lines was the introduction (subtle, we thought, not so subtle she thought) of a younger friend of ours at NPR to Steve's brother Glenn. It worked! And my friend Kitty became my sister-in-law. Talk about a happy ending, especially for me.

It's important to have women with enough seniority and clout to be able to keep the bosses' feet to the fire, pointing out the absence of women in high places, or of opportunities for younger women. Nobody's done that better than my buddy Carole Simpson at ABC, but all of us old girls apply the pressure from time to time, though you still have to be careful not to push too hard or too often. We now have a woman in charge of the Washington Bureau at ABC and the place is actually somewhat sane — something no news organization's ever been accused of in the past. It's remarkable how humor, sympathy, efficiency and collegiality emanating from the top trickles down through an institution. But if it's made a difference for me to have Robin Sproul as my boss, I think she'd say that it's made a difference for her to have people like Carole and me among her troops. We can speak from long experience in the world of working women, and also in the world of working moms. So many of the younger women come to us to counsel them on how to do it — how to strike the balance of work and family. For some, depending on their circumstances, the answer has been, you better take some time at home, the balance isn't working. For others, the fact that we've successfully raised now-adult children while achieving professional success gives them great hope.

Role models do matter, but so do plain old-fashioned, homey how-to suggestions. In the course of a day, I'll find myself going from an interview about the situation in Iraq to a conversation about a colleague's baby's tummy troubles. After a few times of hearing both me and the doctor say things like, "Cheese, bananas, and rice," the young women stop bothering the doctor and just check in with the experienced mothers. It's a role, of course, that women have always played for each other — grandmothers, aunts, mothers, mothers-in-law were on hand on the farm or in the village. As younger generations moved to the suburbs or away altogether, they lost or ignored the wisdom of older women, so Dr. Spock and his successors took over from grandmother as child rearing became an occupation for "professionals." Ironically, it's in the thoroughly modern workplace where women of different generations are reconnecting.

What's so special about these stories? Not a thing. Don't all friends have these experiences? Yes, that's the point. Women rely on friends. If you're lucky like me, you have a built-in best friend called a husband, but I will always need my female friends, and I think most women do. We simply can't exist without the connections to other women. That's where we draw sustenance and find safety. We can count on our women friends when we need a good laugh or a good cry. Women have always known this, as they found ways to cover vast distances in order to congregate — to share their tasks with other women on the pretense of efficiency, but in fact, because we've known through the centuries that when we're together we have more fun.

REPORTER

Outside of the senate family gallery hangs an old oil painting of the meeting of the Electoral Commission of 1876, assembled in the Senate Chamber to decide the validity of ballots in the presidential election. Women fill the press gallery in the picture, and a guide on an adjoining wall conveniently identifies each of them, with the newspapers they represented. Why, I wondered aloud one day, were there more women in the press gallery in 1876 than in 1976? By 1996, when I was asking this question, women were beginning to fill the places again. The guard who overheard me answered, "Because they could write." Well, sure, they could write in 1976, too, but not many papers gave them the chance. Then the guard patiently explained that it wasn't creative writing he was talking about, it was handwriting. Women practiced better penmanship than men, so those elegant-looking ladies in the press gallery were essentially stenographers, not reporters. What a disappointment!

That experience set me off on a little expedition into history, in an attempt to learn more about the women journalists who came before me. And what an eye opener it turned out to be, starting with the story of Mary Katherine Goddard, publisher of the *Maryland Journal*. Though she produced the big scoop on the Battle of Bunker Hill, she's come down through history for her printing rather than her reporting. We all know that the Declaration of Independence was approved on July 4, 1776, but it took a while for the revolutionaries to get up the courage to sign their names to the incendiary document, and a while longer to publish and promulgate it. By the time Congress ordered the distribution of the Declaration, in January 1777, the British had run the legislators out of Philadelphia and into Baltimore. There they took the printing job to the leading newspaper publisher, Mary Katherine Goddard. Printers normally affixed their initials to their work, much the way a union "bug" might mark a document today, but understanding the significance of what she was doing, Goddard signed her full name as the printer of the Declaration of Independence.

Out of seventy-eight papers in the American colonies, sixteen were edited by women. I would guess we haven't come anywhere near that percentage since then. Some of those early women writers were already on their soapboxes — advocating equal education for women, railing against corruption in high places. One of them, Anne Newport Royall, called the "Grandma of Muckrakers" by a biographer, was actually convicted in 1829 of the crime of being a "common scold." Can you imagine if such a charge existed today? We'd all be in trouble. A couple of newspapermen paid her ten-dollar fine to preserve "the honor of the press." The most famous story about Anne Newport Royall might be too good to be true. Desperate for an interview with President John Quincy Adams, the story goes, she caught him swimming in the Potomac River and sat on his clothes until he agreed to talk. The thought of the thoroughly priggish Adams, a man totally unworthy of his mother, Abigail, in my view, shivering in his birthday suit before this somewhat wild newspaperwoman, gives me such a giggle that I hope it happened.

Some of the nineteenth-century women in journalism became household names. Mary E. Clemmer Ames (they all seemed to have multiple names) wrote a weekly "Woman's Letter from Washington" for the *New York* Independent and then the *Brooklyn Daily*

Union. In 1869, her last year at the Brooklyn paper, she made the princely sum of five thousand dollars. (Almost one hundred years later, when I was working on a New York newsletter, my salary wasn't much more than that.) Most famous of all was Nellie Bly (born Elizabeth Jane Cochran) who started working at the *Pittsburgh Gazette* when she was either eighteen or twenty-one — she seems to have been accurate about almost everything but her age. The paper hired her after she sent a well-written letter to the editor supporting women's rights. But her fame came as an investigative reporter for the *New York World* when she feigned insanity to get into the asylum on Blackwell's Island in order to expose the abuses there. The episode serves as a forerunner of today's hidden-camera controversy. To capitalize on her notoriety, in 1889 the *World* sponsored a contest challenging Nellie Bly to go around the world in fewer than Phileas Fogg's eighty days. Readers guessed exactly how long it would take her, and almost one million people submitted entries. The answer: Seventy-two days, six hours, eleven minutes, and fourteen seconds for a trip by ship, train, horse, and burro. Brass bands, fireworks, and parades met her special train from San Francisco to New York, the last leg of her journey. The whole country knew Nellie Bly, and cared enough to come out to cheer her on. Her celebrity certainly outdistanced that of any television star today.

During thirty-six years Nellie Bly wrote more than six hundred newspaper articles, including her coverage of World War I from the Eastern Front. Since she stayed in Vienna even after the U.S. entered the war, appealing through her articles for aid to Austrian war widows and orphans, she was investigated by U.S. military intelligence as a possible enemy agent. The conclusion: "She is outspoken in her opinions going to the extent of being aggressive and defiant." Her great sin, it seems, was attempting to warn the Allies about the dangers of Bolshevism. When she returned to New York after the war, the *Evening Journal* hired her as an advice columnist. Nellie Bly's space in the paper soon became a social services clearinghouse, a place for her to badger the authorities on behalf of her readers.

While Nellie Bly was filing daily stories from her round-the-world adventure, Ida B. Wells was busy acquiring a share of the *Memphis Free Speech and Headlight*. It was a small paper and this fiery young woman, who had been born a slave, was ready to use part of her salary as a schoolteacher to buy into it. She had already contributed many articles on racial injustice to journals around the country, under the pseudonym "Iola." Now she was writing under her own byline, and her newspaper accounts of poor school conditions for black children got her fired from the job. That was nothing compared to her anti-lynching campaign, which resulted in a white mob storming the *Free Speech* offices and destroying the presses. Wells, who was in New York at the time, was warned never to return to Memphis. Undeterred, she kept writing, selling the *Free Speech*'s circulation list for part ownership of the *New York Age*. She attacked white male "chivalry" with her scathing, "No one who reads the record, as it is written on the faces of the million mulattoes in the South, will for a minute conceive that the southern white man had a very chivalrous regard for the honor due women of his race or respect for the womanhood which circumstances placed in his power." Her crusade against lynching took her on a European lecture tour, where she learned about women's civic institutions. When she returned to America, Wells left the newspaper business behind her, taking her crusade for justice into politics, where she organized the first black women's suffrage organization and was one of the founders of the NAACP.

By insisting that only women journalists could cover her press conferences, Eleanor Roosevelt did a lot to promote their position; then the lead-up to World War II and the war itself brought women to a more prominent place in the press corps. But it was a struggle the whole way. Anne O'Hare McCormick, the first woman to serve on the *New York Times* editorial board, wrote most of her groundbreaking reports as a freelancer because the *Times* publisher just couldn't bring himself to hire her. Hers is a remarkable story. Her father abandoned his wife and three daughters, leaving her mother to support the family by running a dry-goods store and going door-to-door selling poetry, of all things. Somehow she managed to send Anne to college and gave her the grounding for a job as associate editor of the *Catholic Universe Bulletin*. After Anne O'Hare married, she accompanied her husband on his many business trips and started sending back reports on what she observed to the *New York Times*. Though the paper readily printed her dispatches, Arthur Ochs refused to hire her, saying, "We have almost a prohibition against women on our editorial staff." So her famous interviews with Hitler, Stalin, Mussolini, and Roosevelt, her warnings about the rise of fascism, all appeared as the work of a freelance reporter. When Ochs died, the *Times* finally put her on the payroll at the age of fifty-six. The next year, 1937, Anne O'Hare McCormick became the first woman writing for a major newspaper to win the prestigious Pulitzer Prize. (A woman student had previously won the prize in a onetime only award to a student newspaper.)

The great World War II correspondent, Helen Kirkpatrick, faced similar problems getting hired on the home front. After she graduated from college in 1931, the editor of the *New York Herald Tribune* gave her a bleak assessment of career prospects for women in journalism, so she went to work at Macy's instead. (The *Current Biography* of 1941 calls work at the department store "often a temporary stopover for bright college graduates.") After a few years there, she returned to the field she had studied in college — international relations — and took a job in Geneva, Switzerland, for the Foreign Policy Association. There she started writing, and newspapers started printing what she wrote. She became influential on the American lecture circuit, wrote a book, then moved to London, where she published a weekly news digest read by all the British leaders. Even after all of this, and another weighty book, she was told by the publisher of the *Chicago Daily News* that he didn't hire women for the foreign desk. "I can't change my sex, but you can change your policy," she told him, and he did. Her first story as a staffer in 1939: an interview with the Duke of Windsor, something her male colleagues claimed couldn't be done; the duke would not talk to the press. As World War II heated up, Kirkpatrick filed three and four times a day for a column syndicated in twenty-four newspapers. Her war coverage, including her vivid descriptions of the London blitz, became so popular that the *Daily News* started putting her picture on their trucks as an advertisement for the paper. When Edward R. Murrow tried to hire her, CBS News told him no more women, so he took on cub reporter Charles Collingwood instead. The only woman to serve on the correspondents' committee planning coverage of the Normandy invasion, Helen Kirkpatrick crossed France with the French Second Armored Division and set up a news bureau in Paris. At war's end she covered the Nuremberg trials from her position as the *New York Post*'s European correspondent. Then, at age forty-five, and probably exhausted, she got married and retired.

Many women reporters didn't have a choice about retiring. After the war they found themselves in a "Rosie the Reporter" situation. They were forced to give up their jobs when the men came home. One was Dorothy Jurney, the assistant city editor of the *Washington News*, who was told in 1946 to train a cub reporter, a returning soldier, to replace her. She moved to Miami, where she resigned herself to abandoning hard news for the women's pages. But she soon found that she was able to have a good deal of impact there by covering such issues as housing needs in the black community. A move to the *Detroit Free Press* as the women's editor gave her more opportunities to assign stories on women's pension rights, women professors' tenure battles, and women as political candidates. Reporters around the country started using the women's pages for serious topics, so newspapers shifted gears, stopped separating out news for women, and started calling the sections "Style" or "Living" so that serious news affecting women effectively disappeared. When an editor of the *New York Times* was called on this question several years ago, he justified the absence of women from his news columns by saying, "We don't cover tea parties." The women of the *Times* instantly had a campaign-style pin made that showed a teapot with a slash through it. It's been on my office wall ever since.

After World War II, some war correspondents stayed on. Most notably, Pauline Frederick, who had been advised by a boss to "stay away from radio, it doesn't like women." Fortunately, she ignored him and NBC hired her. It was for the North American Newspaper Alliance that she covered the war and the Nuremberg trials, and then she went to ABC, where she appeared as the first woman news reporter on television at the 1948 Democratic Convention. Later, back at NBC, her renown grew with her regular program *Pauline Frederick Reporting* and as the United Nations correspondent. In 1976 she was picked as the first woman to moderate a televised presidential debate. Finally, she wrote news analysis for National Public Radio. There she was, this icon, and I would see her in the ladies' room.

I have had the privilege of knowing and working with a good many of the women who battled in this business until the law finally took their side. Nancy Dickerson, the first female TV correspondent for CBS, could not have been kinder to me in the 1960s when I was just starting out and she was one of the most powerful people in

Washington. The women of the *New York Times*, Nan Robertson and Eileen Shanahan and Maggie Hunter, were my husband's colleagues but my heroines. They took on the Great Gray Lady of the *Times* in a suit that embarrassed the paper into paying attention to its women — its correspondents, its secretaries, its women workers at every level. One of Washington's great reporters, Mary McGrory, was told by the *Times* bureau chief that she would be asked to work on the switchboard if she worked there. Women at *Newsweek* and *Time* took similar chances with their bosses, to the benefit of all the women who came after them.

Women fighting for an equal place in journalism also took on the established journalistic institutions that excluded women from their ranks. Back in 1868 journalist Jane Cunningham Croly organized the women's club, Sororis, after she had been barred from a New York Press Club dinner. Things hadn't changed one iota a hundred years later at the National Press Club. No women members were accepted, and women covering events there were forced to stew and sweat together in the balcony while the men sat in an air-conditioned room below, enjoying a meal. It was not until 1971, after much organized agitation, that women were admitted as full members.

Women like me owe eternal debts of gratitude to the women who pitched fits in print journalism, and the women in broadcasting like Marlene Sanders and Barbara Walters who went before us. It must have been incredibly difficult for them because it was plenty tough for me when I was starting out — men told me how women couldn't broadcast news because our voices weren't authoritative enough, how women couldn't be writers at news magazines because men would have to work for us, how women couldn't be counted on to stay in a job because we would go off and have babies. It's important to understand that when this was happening to me and to other women my age, we had no idea it was happening to anyone else, as it was in almost every profession. I'm sure some of my contemporaries understood that we were being wildly discriminated against, but it took me and — I've learned in later years — my good friends a while to get it.

I remember it so well. After college I had gotten a job through the placement office — no kidding. A family of Wellesley women, headed by the indomitable Sophie Altman, produced a series of TV shows out of Washington. They hired me to help with the main production, *It's Academic*, a high school quiz-kids show that's still thriving in Washington. Local versions of the program aired around the country, and as the show was picked up by more stations, I helped produce it in the new cities. Mrs. Altman had also for many years produced a program on the local NBC station called *Teen Talk*, which, coincidentally, I had appeared on as a teenager. While I was working there, the station decided that the show had run its course, but the managers still wanted Altman Productions to come up with another public service program to fulfill its licensing requirements. The solution: a program that brought the huge community of foreign correspondents in Washington on to the public airwaves and in touch with American public officials. It was called *Meeting of the Minds* and I was its anchor. I was twenty-one. Of course I had never done anything like it before, but I think I was too young and dumb to be scared, and the guests and journalists treated me well — after all, they wanted to be on TV. As the program that preceded the old standby, *Meet the Press*, it was watched by all of official Washington.

My old friend Roger Wilkins, the civil rights leader and historian, tells a funny story about that. He served as assistant attorney general in the Johnson administration, but for some reason LBJ had gotten it in his head that Wilkins might be in Bobby Kennedy's camp, which to Johnson was the ultimate disloyalty. Roger appeared as a guest on my program and did a masterful defense of Johnson's civil rights record. The president saw the program and from there on out Roger was always in his good graces.

When I finally convinced Steven to marry me (he jokes that his proposal was "Oh, all right, Cokie"), it never occurred to me to try to keep my job, even though I was making more money than he was. I, of course, just said good-bye and headed to New York, where he was working. Then I started looking. And I was appalled. Men were so blatant in their "We don't hire women" statements — one of them even delivered that Olympian judgment with his hand on my thigh — that it was truly shocking. But there was no one to share the shock. Steven didn't think what I was telling him was particularly odd, the world for men and women had never been the same, why would it be now? He probably thought I was exaggerating anyway. All that he knew for sure was that I kept failing to snare employment. Fortunately, I couldn't type or take shorthand. Many women of my era graduated from fine schools like

Wellesley, Smith, and Vassar and then went on to secretarial school at Katie Gibbs. It was my view that learning clerical skills could stick you forever in a clerical job. I know people for whom that hasn't been true, but I also know plenty for whom it has been. I will never advise a young woman even in this day and age to "come in the door" as a secretary. Everybody needs secretaries so desperately that a person good at it is trapped, a person bad at it is branded as a lousy worker.

At one point in this job search, I lost my temper. It was clear I had nothing to lose; the man interviewing me thought I was speaking Swahili when I suggested that women might, in fact, be writers for his news magazine. He kept talking to me about all the female researchers and what great jobs they did and how much they loved it there. (I was not even slightly a feminist at this point, but I had been raised in the South and I knew an "Our servants are so close, they are actually members of our family" statement when I heard one.) I allowed as how I thought my credentials went beyond researcher status and that men who had graduated in my year from comparable schools were thriving at his magazine. He was so chagrined at this conversation that he didn't know how to deal with it; I was challenging his eternal verities. Men did one thing, women did another. What was the problem? Many, many years later this man was up for an important job at NPR when I had become someone who could make a difference in his employment. I didn't think he had any memory whatsoever of our long-ago conversation and I didn't rat on him to the search committee. I decided they could figure out on their own that he was not the right person for our organization.

When I finally did get a job writing for a weekly newsletter, I loved it. Reporting is, after all, a license to snoop, and you get paid to learn something new every day and then tell the world about it. It's not necessarily the most mature of vocations, with the instant gratification of being able to see your story in the paper, hear and see your broadcast on radio and TV on a daily basis, but it is fun. Before we moved to Greece in 1974, I went around to the networks asking them to use me if they could, saying that I was studying the language and would have access to Steve's Telex machine. Everyone expressed some interest; CBS actually gave me a tape recorder to take with me. I planned to get the family settled and then start pitching stories. Well, no sooner had we moved into our house and placed the kids in schools than war broke out in Cyprus. Steve was summoned to the island, where he was frighteningly out of touch for several days. By the time he came home I was a seasoned radio reporter, filing every hour. I had even learned to rely on my five-year-old son as a source; he had counted the number of tanks heading up the main avenue out of Athens. On the day the military regime fell and democracy returned to Greece, my report, which I filed from a flower stall outside the presidential palace, led the *CBS Evening News.* Finally, there could be no question that I had well and truly broken into journalism.

When I returned to Washington, the world had changed in the eleven years since I had left. Women were in a considerably better position. And at National Public Radio women were in prime positions. Part of the reason for that was the payscale, i.e., low. It was easier to get good women to work for low wages than good men. Also the network started from scratch in 1972, so there weren't men already in place who would have to be replaced if women were hired to cover such subjects as the Supreme Court and Congress and candidates. People often ask me whether I have trouble getting interviews because I am a woman. As far as I know, the answer to that question is no. Politicians care much more about the initials after your name — NPR, ABC — than the letters before it — Mr. or Ms. I've always joked that a news organization with a wide enough circulation could send a two-headed monster to interview a politician and the only response would be, "Would you like a cup of coffee, or perhaps two cups?" They know my interviews will be seen and heard by millions of people, even if I am wearing a skirt.

At some point, being a woman became an advantage, at least for some of us. When women viewers and listeners and readers started objecting to the all-white-male casts of characters presented to them on program after program, the tables turned. Producers and editors actively looked for women for their broadcasts and broadsheets. Or at least they looked for one woman. That would do it. Nina Totenberg tells the story of having an editor tell her, "But, Nina, we already have our woman." ABC News would probably never have come looking for me had I been a man. The network thought it needed a woman, at least occasionally, on the round-table at the end of the Brinkley program. The producers had tried a few but hadn't settled on anyone, so someone suggested me and it worked. But it wasn't because I was a woman that ten years later I ended up as the co-anchor of the broadcast.

To hear many men tell it, women are getting all the jobs, taking them away from the people to whom they naturally belong, men. Baloney. Usually we still find ourselves fighting, if not to get in, at least to move up. How often have you seen a TV program where everyone on it is a woman? I must say, it really ticks me off when someone says, "Oh, she only got that job because she's a woman," as Washington wags did about Madeleine Albright, for instance. Talk about no-win situations. You spend the first half of your working life being told you can't have a job because you're a woman and the second half being told you got the job only because you're a woman. Give me a break!

Now the women who went through the experience of being shut out of the good jobs have moved up in the world of work. But we all remember what we went through, and how our experiences changed the landscape. Katharine Graham reveals in her wonderful book that she had trouble as a woman even though she was the boss at the *Washington Post*. It was when women started sharing the stories of our struggles that the modern women's movement got its momentum. We went into the workplace as a group, an entire generation of educated women that was determined to break down barriers for ourselves and the women who came after us, and we have the scratches and bruises to show for it. But it mattered. It mattered for us as individuals and it also mattered to the institutions we infiltrated to hear women's voices.

Take journalism as an example. Look at the things women wrote about — remember Nellie Bly highlighting the problems of divorce and slum life and the plight of war widows and orphans and ending her journalistic days with a social services column. None of the men writing at the time noticed, as Anne O'Hare McCormick did, that after two world wars in Europe more women had survived than men and women were left to clean up the mess. McCormick campaigned for more female representation at the San Francisco Conference that established the United Nations. And then there was Dorothy Jurney and her contemporaries who used the women's pages to underline women's problems. It's still happening today. Women journalists write more about women politicians and issues affecting families and children, whether it's about breast cancer research or hardships in child care, or overcrowding in schools.

We also brought a different sensibility to political reporting, for better or for worse. When there were only "boys on the bus," male reporters covering male candidates for office, no one ever considered a politician's behavior toward women relevant to his ability to do the job. When women joined the campaign caravans, they did think it made a difference. Gary Hart's peccadilloes were something women in newsrooms kept puzzling over. How could we deal with it? We thought it mattered, but there were no roadmaps for this kind of coverage. Then Hart made it easy by throwing down the gauntlet to follow him, and the *Miami Herald* did. A lot of people are sorry that we now know so much about a presidential candidate's private life. I'm not among them. I think character counts, especially for a president, who serves in a singular position, who does not have the check of ninety-nine other senators or four hundred and thirty-four other members of the House. And I think that attitudes toward women and family contribute to the definition of character.

The real point here is that we need diversity in newsrooms. We need people of different ages, races, sexes, and interests so that all kinds of ideas come to the table. We have made great strides along those lines since I started out more than thirty years ago. We also need diversity in boardrooms where the bottom-line decisions are made. Don't hold your breath.

CIVIL RIGHTS
ACTIVIST

"So many people ask me, 'How do you deal with so many different things?' But from my viewpoint, there was a central core to all of it. And if you follow it, really, it's always advancing women." That's what Dorothy Height's been doing for the last sixty-some years, and at age eighty-six she's still doing it. After forty years at the helm, she stepped up from her daily duties as president of the National Council of Negro Women to chairman of the organization at the end of last year. That meant she finally had a few minutes to sit down with me for a look back at her place at center stage of the struggle for civil rights and a look ahead at the fight for the future.

Strategically located between the White House and the Capitol, hers is the only building, Ms. Height told me, owned by African-Americans in downtown Washington, D.C. She put together the financing for the historic old structure with a loan guaranteed by General Motors, Ford, and Chrysler. And though it's been an effort to raise the money to pay for it, it's worth it because "our women's groups have been very conscious of the importance of having someplace you can claim as your own." Dorothy Height, still elegantly erect in a gray suit and matching felt hat, can claim that place of her own in history.

By the time Ms. Height achieved national notice as a leader in the civil rights movement, she was already a well-known figure here in Washington. My family cared deeply about civil rights; it had been a cause of consternation politically and morally all of our lives, and we knew many of the activists in the movement. But I also knew Dorothy Height because she and my mother had worked together on several projects — they were part of a cadre of women who seemed to run Washington. They ran welfare programs through Family and Child Services, they ran employment for the handicapped through Goodwill Industries, they established the first homes for abandoned and abused women in the House of Ruth. They used women's clubs to accomplish whatever social service program they thought was needed at that moment. Dorothy Height had been doing that ever since she was a little girl growing up in Rankin, Pennsylvania, where her father was a builder, her mother a private nurse.

It was at a time, early in this century, when the "women's club movement" was at its apex. In the decades after the Civil War, white women across the country organized to share common interests and community involvement. Under the leadership of activists like Ida B. Wells, black women soon followed suit, creating their own clubs. Some were devoted to study, many were devoted to service, all gave women the opportunity to work — and presumably, gossip — together. (These societies were not always viewed as benign activities. When Julia Ward Howe established the New England Women's Club in 1868, the *Boston Transcript* editorialized that "Homes will be ruined, children neglected, woman is straying from her place." There was reason, in the end, to worry. Out of the club movement grew the suffrage movement, and we know what that did!)

Through her mother's affiliation with the Emma J. Moore Women's Club, Dorothy, at the age of fourteen, became president of the Pennsylvania Girls' Clubs. Her whole childhood seems one of successes — she won a four-year college scholarship from the Elks for her oration on the Constitution — so it was not much of a surprise when Barnard College accepted her application for admission. What happened next, however, did surprise and sear Dorothy Height, wounding her in a way that still causes her to wince as she tells the story.

She arrived at the Barnard dean's office, per instruction, and was kept waiting forever. Finally, she was told to come back in September because "we have a quota of two and we have two Negro students." Think of it, this fifteen-year-old sitting in a scary office in New York City, hearing something so humiliating. Shakily, all these years later, Ms. Height remembers, "Even as I tell it now, I can almost feel it. It was the most traumatic experience. I was afraid to get on the phone and call my mother." An older sister grabbed her by the hand, marched her to the subway and into the registration line at New York University. The dean there took one look at her grades and admitted her instantly. "Well, I tell you. To this moment I loved every moment at NYU," Dorothy Height now says with an appreciative chuckle.

First she studied religion until the head of the department told her, "You need to think of something else, because the church isn't ready for women. And the black church surely isn't ready for you." That's how Dorothy Height became a social worker, a relatively new line of work that had its origins in the settlement house movement, which had grown out of the women's clubs. She finished NYU in three years and got her master's degree in the fourth, then she did more graduate work at Columbia University. Next stop, far from the world of academe: the Brownsville Community Center, in Brooklyn's highest delinquency area. Then "I was recruited by the Department of Welfare, the City of New York, to join that staff. And I left the Brownsville Center, because I couldn't resist twenty-seven fifty a week." After that, it was a job at the Young Women's Christian Association, and it was for life.

Ms. Height tells the story as if it happened yesterday. She was the new staffer at the Harlem Y, so she drew weekend duty. The assignment: escort First Lady Eleanor Roosevelt to a meeting called by Mary McLeod Bethune. So it was that the twenty-five-year-old Dorothy met two of the century's most influential women. It was November 7, 1937, "and as I was leaving, Mrs. Bethune stopped me, and she asked my name. And I told her. And then she said, 'Come back. We need you.' So, I've been back ever since." Back as a worker for the National Council on Negro Women, an organization then headed by Mrs. Bethune. Two years earlier Mrs. Bethune, an adviser on minority affairs to President Roosevelt, had organized the council as a coalition of fourteen black women's groups. (Today 14 national and 250 community-based organizations, representing four million women, fall under the NCNW umbrella.) Dorothy Height found herself working with the Council as a volunteer while doing her paid work for the YWCA, where she moved on to the national staff in 1944.

Her two roles meshed, because the Y was a remarkably progressive organization. Modern women's histories include lines like, "The YWCA was not integrated until 1946." To me the fact that the Y did integrate in 1946 is mind-boggling. Remember the time — separation of the races was legally enforced throughout the South and informally observed in much of the rest of the country; soldiers fighting in World War II did so in segregated units; it was eight years before *Brown* v. *Board of Education* ordered desegregation of the public schools, two years before a civil rights plank was added to the platform of the Democratic Party. Still, in a brave move, the Y decided that to be true to its Christian principles it must endorse equality of the races. The staff, with the assistance of Dorothy Height, helped write the interracial charter the YWCA convention in 1946 would be called upon to adopt. She recalls that, as the meeting was set to convene, 210 associations resisted the idea of integration, saying, "Given our Christian purpose, it's a thing we should do. But if we do it, we will go out of existence in our community. We will have no white members."

Trying to give some sense of the drama, Ms. Height recounts the lobbying of the various Y chapters by the leadership, and then the stirring keynote address by Dr. Benjamin Mays, then president of Morehouse College, an all-black institution: " 'I hear you say that the time is not ripe. But the time is always ripe to do justice. And if you have a Christian purpose, if the time is not ripe, then it should be your purpose to ripen the time.' It's hard to recapture what happened. Some women from some southern communities walked out. Some left the convention. They said they could not hold their heads up if they stayed and were there for the action." But the charter was adopted and Ms. Height still can hear the president of the organization, as she looked out over the group of three thousand women, asking, " 'Is this going to be easy to do?' And there was a kind of 'no,' as if it had been organized. But that was the turning point. And the YWCA kept moving. And I think one of the things that was so encouraging to me was the leadership of women."

If it was hard to get the women of the YWCA to accept racial equality, it turned out to be even harder to get the men of the civil rights movement to accept women's equality. As the president of the National Council of Negro Women, a post she assumed in 1957, Dorothy Height took her place at the table of the black organizations. (The others and their presidents: the Urban League, Whitney Young; the NAACP, Roy Wilkins; the Student Non-Violent Coordinating Committee, John Lewis; the Southern Christian Leadership Conference, Martin Luther King, Jr.; the Congress of Racial Equality, James Farmer.) At almost every movement meeting she was the only woman in the room. When they started organizing the massive 1963 March on Washington, she started militating for a woman speaker. Now she says with great passion, "It was impossible. We did everything. Their arguments were very clear. 'Women are represented in the NAACP. Women are in the Urban League. Women belong to the churches. Women are in the labor movement. Women are represented.' Here were great champions of justice, and they would say, 'Well, you know how highly we regard you.' " To show their regard, the women were given choice seats for the march; they could be seen but not heard. "The only female voice heard was Mahalia Jackson. And we kept saying, 'We're fighting against this.' I said, 'Everybody thinks that Negroes can sing. But also we want to be able to speak up for ourselves.' " Finally, the women dropped the argument: "We just hit a point where we just had to ride above it because it was so important not to have a great division."

The experience served to reinforce an already well-learned lesson, that women would have to help themselves. And self-help has been the hallmark of the many programs initiated by the NCNW. Basic hunger needed to be addressed, particularly in the Deep South, and the organization came up with an inventive way to make a difference — pig banks. Starting with fifty-five Yorkshire pigs, families in Sunflower County, Mississippi, were able to become self-sustaining. As part of the program sponsored by the council, experts went to Mississippi to tend to the health of the pigs, and they ended up serving the families as well — teaching them about preventive medicine, good eating habits, and hygiene. Something as simple as pigs led to better medical care and education for those families. It's hard to imagine a group of men being willing to operate on so humble a scale.

The self-help theme also underlies the Black Family Reunions that Dorothy Height's organization started in 1986. They bring together black Americans in cities all over the country, where people enjoy one another's company, good food, and good music, and also learn about health, home-ownership, and higher education. "It has been amazing, over that period we've had some fourteen million people in eight cities without a single police incident," she says with some satisfaction. "The emphasis is on traditional values and on our coping skills and helping people get a sense of stressing the community as more of an extended family. That's what supported many of us as we were growing up, the fact that everybody in the community looked out for you." The community looked out for the children because the parents, mother and father, were at work. Dorothy Height finds all of this agonizing in the white community about working outside the home a little silly, as she has for some time. When Ms. Height served on President Kennedy's Commission on the Status of Women, she had to remind her white sisters that their experiences were not universal. "I remember that as we were coming down to our conclusions that said something like 'Women grow up, become adolescents, go into the labor force, get married, come out of the labor force and have their children, go back in the labor force.' And I said, 'That sounds to me like another world. That's not the African-American woman.' "

Black women worked for pay and they worked for free, taking on double duty in the work force and the volunteer force, plus, of course, the home force. With some indignation Ms. Height insists, "There's a myth that we don't volunteer. We've only survived because we volunteer. We have provided for ourselves so much that our white sisters take for granted. I remember when I worked at the Harlem Y. After a year, I was put in charge of the residence. There was not a bed in the city of New York in 1938 for a black unwed mother. Yet we had Florence Crittendon homes (for white unwed mothers) all over the city. Those little club groups, they provided those services." Little club groups like her mother had been part of, and she had known as a girl, then used as an adult

— those were the social service agencies blacks had to depend on.

They still do, many through programs initiated by the NCNW. But Dorothy Height sees great urgency to do more: "The fastest entries into the correction system now are girls, a 23 percent increase. And many who are incarcerated have two to three children. So, I think that much more attention needs to be given. That's why we put the stress on the family." And to pay attention to young black girls at a time when the nation seems focused on young black males. "I'm not saying we don't need to put stress on the black male, but we need a stress on our young women as well. They are the ones who are left with the families. So, I think we have to use every strategy that we can to reinforce those who are trying to make it. There are so many who are underachieving because of their frustration. They don't see a life for themselves. That's why I think that we have to offer every opportunity, every incentive, to encourage our young women."

By doing that, Ms. Height's convinced, the whole society will prosper even though men don't believe it. Looking back over her many years in the fray, she says emphatically, "The advances of women have always advanced men." A prime example: a case in the Philadelphia post office, where women couldn't lift the heavy bags, so men said they shouldn't have the jobs. "Men shouldn't have been lifting them either," she recalls with a laugh, "they had hernias and all from it. We said, 'If you can put a man on the moon, there ought to be some way to lift those.' Well, they got ways of electronically doing that. That advanced it for men. And I think a lot of men don't understand that." There's an understatement.

Dorothy Height has spent a lifetime understating and conciliating, but she's beginning to get a little impatient with both these days. She'd like to hear some more of the righteous indignation that formed the core of the civil rights movement, expressed so eloquently during the March on Washington. And she believes it's women who are likely to be more righteously indignant. "We had strong leadership among men. But I think that women when they get on something, we don't give up easily." Lord knows she hasn't.

WIFE

When Steve and I got married in 1966, one of the most useful wedding presents we received was *Webster's Third New International Dictionary*, unabridged. The hefty tome has served us well as it's traveled around the world with us. Out of curiosity, I recently looked up the word *wife* in it. First definition? "Woman." That pretty much sums up the attitude of 1966: to be a woman was to be a wife. The dictionary goes on to list other meanings under the primary definition: "a woman acting in a specified capacity . . . one who sells something . . . (a fishwife) . . . one who has charge of something . . . (henwife) . . . a woman worker (washerwife)." Never does that most-used term, "housewife," appear. I suppose it was considered tautological at the time. Not until the second definition do we get "a married woman."

Why am I surprised? After all, the celebrant at the marriage ceremony itself declared us "man and wife." Isn't that saying the same thing, to be a woman is to be a wife? I certainly thought so. Even the nuns who taught me, for whom I had great affection and respect, called themselves "brides to Christ." My goal in life was marriage, then motherhood. I wanted to get married as soon as possible after college, do something interesting for a while, but have babies as fast as I could. Then I thought I would stay home, do good things in the community, and enhance my husband's career. That's what suburban life in the 1950s seemed to dictate, and I believed then and believe now that it's a worthy way to spend a life. It's what my friends' mothers did, although, interestingly, not what my own mother did. It's what any man I could expect to marry would certainly expect.

Steven and I never had that conversation, we never even thought about it. When we met, in the summer of 1962, at the ages of eighteen and nineteen, the subject wasn't on the table. It's about the only one that wasn't — since we were at a student political convention in Columbus, Ohio. Debates raged fiercely over racism and imperialism and capitalism; no one had heard of sexism. When we went back to school and eventually started dating nothing mattered but young love. As we started to "get serious" only two topics disturbed our reverie: how could we reconcile our religious differences, and when would he bite the bullet and marry me? Debating the religion question — he's Jewish, I'm Catholic — served to concentrate our minds on how we felt about family and how we envisioned our lives unfolding. Those late-adolescent agonies at times seemed unfixable. But a lot of tearful conversations and a little growing up helped us come to an agreement about how we would handle religion, then it was just a question of getting Steven to pop the question. After all, I was twenty-two years old, watching "the best years of my life" just swirl down the drain. Finally, after I threatened to "go to California," which sounded to me like a realistic version of Timbuktu, he proposed. The setting, or more to the point, the setup, was a carriage ride in Central Park. We were almost out of the park by the time he finally said the magic words, not that I'm still holding that against him after all these years.

As to the religion part, the solution in retrospect seems simple. And the process of coming to it shaped the way we handled many future difficulties. We chose the path of inclusion, not exclusion. We practice both religions. We were married in an ecumenical ceremony in the garden of the home I hold so dear. The children were raised in both religious traditions, learning more about religion than many kids of their era, and celebrating Christian and Jewish holidays. It can get a little expensive and more than a little exhausting at certain seasons but it's worked. In all our married years not one argument has been over religion. I can't say the same about work. We've had many a "heated discussion," as the politicians say, over the appropriate allocation of each other's time between work and family.

Not only did the rules change on the state of modern American matrimony just as we were entering into it, our own expectations, especially my own expectations, changed as well. But never comfortably. Most domestic debates dealing with my role as wife have stemmed from my own ambivalence and overriding guilt, feeling wherever I was I should have been someplace else. When we got married, we never even talked about my job situation. Even though I loved anchoring the TV show and it was a great opportunity for such a young woman, we both took it for granted that I would quit and move to New York with Steven, and so did everyone else, including my own mother, who has always worked. I assumed that having achieved my goal, having been awarded the title "wife," I would settle into a bower of bliss.

What we settled into instead was a rent-controlled apartment on the West Side near what was then "Needle Park." When we arrived there after our honeymoon, a sign in the elevator read "No heat or hot water until further notice." And if Steven had tried to carry me across the threshold, he would have had a rough time because the previous tenants had taken up the floor in a fit of New York nastiness. I did love playing house — furnishing the apartment, making things pretty, cooking grown-up meals in our miserable little kitchen. But my efforts to create "home sweet home" were thwarted by my cash flow. Until I went to work, we had to stretch Steve's salary to cover two. As my attempts to find a job strung out for weeks, then months, we decided we better put a halt to most purchases. Because I hated asking my parents for money, I had always baby-sat or found odd jobs even as a kid. Now as an adult I felt like I was asking my husband for money. Even though we had a joint checking account, and even though Steven has never been anything but incredibly generous, it made me miserable that all the deposits were his.

It got pretty depressing — getting all dressed up to go sell myself in yet another interview, only to get turned down, and it reached the point where I was ready to do just about anything. But the days without one of those dreaded appointments could be even worse. When winter came on, I discovered that the building superintendent turned off the heat during the day with the clear message that no one should be home. It was cold and it was lonely. I couldn't wait for the day to be over so I could see Steven. Poor boy, loving me wasn't enough, he was supposed to entertain me as well.

In doing some research on marriage, I've discovered that I was simply following in my foremothers' footsteps. In eighteenth-century America, female friends and relatives would help a woman adjust to her new situation, often staying with the young couple for the first months of marriage, making sure the bride met other women, even accompanying them on their wedding trips. Can you imagine anyone trying that in this day and age? By the early nineteenth century, writers describe "marriage trauma," where women sank into depression at the prospect of becoming someone's mate. They seemed to understand better than my generation did what it would mean to lose independence. Letters and diaries from the period make these women sound downright desperate. One wrote her fiancé, "Every joy in anticipation depends on you, and from you must I derive every pleasure." In the latter part of the century, as women became educated, many opted out of marriage altogether. According to historian Sara Evans, nearly half of all college-educated women in the late nineteenth century never married.

Maybe it would have made a difference if I had known any of that when I was a newlywed. I doubt that I would have believed it. Now that I look back on that time, I realize what useful, if painful, lessons it provided. I learned that I need the company of other women. I learned that I perform much better with the discipline of a schedule. And I learned that I derive tremendous satisfaction from my work. I'm not particularly proud of those realizations. I think a more creative and self-contained person would do better on her own. But I'm awfully glad I found out about myself when I did. Fortunately, I had known Steven so long and loved him so much that I didn't even entertain the thought that marriage might be a mistake. Suppose I had not had that experience then, had not found out that I need work in order to be fulfilled? I probably would have discovered it after my first baby was born, and then I would have been truly tied up in knots about whether I was a failure as a mother.

When I finally did get a job at a small business newsletter in New York, I became a much happier human being. Steve probably became a much happier person as well, but he was nice enough not to tell me I had been driving him crazy. Still, there was no doubt that my work was secondary, something for me to do, not something that would merit any consideration in family decision making. My sweet husband still blushes when I remind him of a story from that time. He was extolling the virtues of living on the West Side of Manhattan, only one express subway stop from Times Square. "Now," he mused, "if I worked in the building where *Esquire* magazine is, for instance, then it would probably make sense to live on the East Side." In randomly picking a building as an example, he had unthinkingly chosen the exact place where I worked. It was one of those sensitive male moments. And, yes, getting to my job was a pain in the neck.

It clearly was taking some getting used to, this idea that we were two, not one, and that we had responsibility for each other. Early one morning the phone rang and the operator asked if we knew anyone in Oberlin, Ohio, who might have called us; they were having trouble identifying the calling number for billing purposes. I said no and hung up. Steven groggily asked who called, I told him, and he protested, "But we do know someone in Oberlin, my brother goes to school there." "Yes," I responded, "but if the phone company can't figure out its billing, that's its problem." After I went to work I called Steve as a joke, disguised my voice, and said, "Mr. Roberts, did you lie to our operator this morning?" "No," he gulped, "that was my wife, C-O-K . . ." As I burst out laughing, he knew he'd been caught.

The newsletter where I was working folded and I landed at a local television station in a job I didn't like very much. By the time I caught on it wasn't the place for me, I was pregnant, much to my delight. I stayed until the baby was born, then quit. No such thing as maternity leave existed. The day we brought Lee home from the hospital, past the piles of uncollected garbage on the streets because of the sanitation workers' strike and the gaggles of schoolkids out on the streets because of the teachers' strike, the *New York Times* assigned Steven to Los Angeles. Neither of us had ever been there, but to me it had all the earmarks of a great adventure. Off into the sunset with my handsome husband and precious baby. The old Ford Falcon that carried us across the country didn't exactly have the look of a shining chariot, but we did land on a Malibu mountaintop overlooking the Pacific Ocean. Farewell, Needle Park, hello, Lotus Land.

Hibiscus and bougainvillea replaced the garbage-strewn streets and we settled into a romantic idyll. Except there were diapers and bottles. And Steve was away a lot of the time. In those days, the roles could not have been more clear. Steven's work came first. He would do what he could to accommodate me and the baby, but within the parameters of the job. Fortunately, my old boss Sophie Altman had just sold *It's Academic* to the local NBC affiliate. It worked out perfectly for everyone to have me produce the show out there, rather than fly someone out from Washington all the time. It gave me something to do, someplace to go, some people to meet, and some checks to cash. That was the way both of us saw it. Most of the tapings were on weekends, when Steven often baby-sat. Otherwise, it was catch as catch can with child care, just as it is for most people still. Lots of friends and family came to visit, so I didn't feel lonely. I think some motherhood hormones must have kicked in as well because I was happy as could be. We even managed from time to time to sneak off on what I called have-an-affair-with-your-wife weekends.

When Lee was not quite two years old, Rebecca arrived. Life grew geometrically more complicated, as I had also taken on a research project on the youth vote for the Twentieth Century Fund. In those years, Steve and I also worked on magazine pieces together where I did most of the research and reporting, he did most of the writing. (I later found out that my mother was quite horrified by one we wrote for the *New York Times Magazine* on venereal disease. How did I know about all those awful things?) Steve became a sort of one-man journalism school for me, generously sharing a byline. Now we do that all the time, but then it was key to my building a body of work. And we were both slowly becoming aware that some-day that would make a difference.

We were not, after all, impervious to the world around us. Quite the contrary, we were reporting on it. That world, particularly in California in the early 1970s, resounded with the chants of revolution — the student movement, the antiwar movement, the black power movement, and the women's movement. Women who were my contemporaries were rising up, declaring their independence from many of society's strictures and institutions, including marriage. Women like me were beginning to voice complaints about our unequal roles, to stir up family arguments on the subject. Men like Steven were defensive on one hand, trying to adapt on the other, taking on more child care when it was convenient, even washing a dish or two. While we were making minuscule adjustments the world was turning topsy-turvy. I remember calling a prominent feminist who was a friend of Steve's for an article we were doing. I wanted to let her know I was married to him, but I was actually afraid to use the word *wife*. She would certainly, in my view, find it a disparaging term. I carefully formulated my sentence to say, "Steve Roberts is my husband." How much times had changed in the not very many years since acquiring the title "wife" had been my life's ambition.

Even with our recently raised consciousness, not a lot changed. When Rebecca was a few days old we were evacuated from our home because of big brush fires. Steve deposited me and the two babies and, fortunately, my mother in a downtown hotel and went out to cover the fires. I had an *It's Academic* taping scheduled that couldn't be canceled. (I had planned the date thinking the baby would not yet have arrived. How was I to know she'd be early?) So, I left the ten-day-old and the two-year-old with my mother in a hotel room and went to work. Mamma said, "When I had a ten-day-old, I was still in the hospital." I, oh so thoughtfully, shot back, "Take her to the hospital if you want, I have to go to work." That's the way it was. If you worked, you accommodated. There was never any question of the workplace or the family accommodating you.

Luckily, I found jobs with schedules that were by and large flexible, and a baby-sitting family of girls that was by and large available. But no matter what I did, it was clear that my main employment was that of wife. Even people in my work world saw it that way. When a children's TV program I was producing was nominated for an Emmy, I received a certificate inscribed with my name. Instead of the name that appeared on the show's credits, "Cokie Roberts," the certificate reads, "Mrs. Stephen [sic] Roberts." That, I think, says it all.

Even so, I was enough of a "working wife" that the editors of the *New York Times* were worried about it when they transferred Steven to Greece. Would I raise a ruckus the way women suddenly were? They didn't want some harridan on their hands, and neither did Steven. But they were safe; it was another adventure as far as I was concerned. The newspaper helped by paying for me to travel with Steve some of the time, which made an enormous difference in my enjoyment of the years abroad. We always have such a good time together, working and laughing and loving our way through all kinds of silly situations. One night way in the east of Turkey we checked in at some godforsaken hotel where no woman had ever stayed. There were no private rooms, just dormitories. The innkeepers put all the other travelers in one dorm and left the other to Steve and me. The only heat came from a coal-burning stove that we were totally incapable of stoking into life. So we took all the blankets from every other bed and huddled together on one narrow mattress. When we woke up we were covered with soot, but we were still having a wonderful time.

In those years I found out something new about this wife business — or maybe more accurately, the husband side of that coin. With Steven away so much, I was forced to deal with the inconveniences of living in a foreign country all on my own. And Greece was in transition — hired help didn't come cheap and time-saving devices didn't exist. I remember one day struggling to cut up a whole chicken, fantasizing about packages of chicken parts. Pretty pathetic. Most of the other American wives there had the backing of some major institution, like the U.S. government or big corporate offices, when they ran into the inevitable culture clashes.

One memorable old world–new reality dustup came when I went to register the family as aliens. We started with Steven's documents, and the bureaucrats asked a series of questions, including, "religion." I told them "Jewish" and they had no problem with that. When we got to my religion, they assumed it would be the same, and were highly confused when I said "Catholic." They approached the line on the children's forms with some trepidation. What, they asked dubiously, were they? When I replied "both," they went nuts. "Impossible," they cried as they disappeared into a back room to thrash it out. I could hear the screams. "The father takes precedence," shouted one. "But he's not Christian," bellowed another. What a terrible choice I had presented them, between patriarchy and Christianity. Much to my amazement, Christianity won out.

By having to do everything myself I found out that I was actually a highly competent human being, which was gratifying. I didn't need Steven around, I wanted him around.

Life was a lot more fun with him than without him. He also provided the anchor for our little brood. Early on, he decreed that Sundays would be family days, no one could accept any invitations or make any commitments. Sometimes we all chafed under that, but it turned out over the decades to be an essential part of our lives together, whether we were picnicking or playing games or pondering the fate of the universe. Emotionally, I had not even the slightest desire to manage on my own, but practically I could do it. That was a revelation. (I did think it was a little much, though, one day when Steve and the landlord sat in the living room drinking brandy while I was in the basement fixing the furnace.) It was also a revelation that I could report on my own. CBS News regularly ran my radio spots, and sometimes TV as well. Several magazines printed my articles. And Steve and I still wrote pieces together, so I kept my name in circulation, which helped considerably when I came back to Washington to start the dread job hunt.

Steven says now that the day my role shifted was the day I went to work at NPR. I would mark it a few weeks earlier than that — somewhere in the period after we got back to Washington and I realized necessity dictated that I have a full-time, well-paying job.

Psychically, I had expected that. I knew Washington was a tough town, where a woman better have an answer to the "what do you do?" question or face ostracism. I hate that, and I think it's ridiculous. But I knew I didn't have the self-confidence to withstand it. What I had not expected was the money crunch. When we were married eleven years earlier, families could easily live on a *New York Times* reporter's salary in our neighborhood or one nearby. By 1977 that was impossible. So, work for me was no longer just a question of my personal satisfaction, where earning "pin money" would do. Now it was real, just like Steve's work.

Soon it was really just like Steve's work. We were covering the same beat, Capitol Hill, and we commuted together, often ate lunch together, and saw each other throughout the day in media mobs. Most of our colleagues knew we were married, of course, but one newcomer whispered to a friend, "Steve Roberts is having an affair with that reporter from National Public Radio." His news organization was more prestigious than mine at the time, and he made more money than I did, but there couldn't be any pretense that his work was more demanding than mine. Neither one of us could say, "You just don't understand, dear." And

Steven couldn't walk in the door at the end of the day and plead for mercy from the worries of household and family. We walked in the door together.

Steven realized just how much our situations had changed when the *New York Times* asked him to go to Three Mile Island, to cover the accident at the nuclear plant. Normally, he would have just gotten in the car and gone, but I was already there, and the kids were nervous about it. He told the *Times* he couldn't do it to the kids, it would totally freak them to have two parents in what they saw as danger. Still, even as Steven was accepting my new role, he would often play on my always-at-the-ready guilt about working too hard. When I was covering the Pope's first visit to this country in 1979, one day I called home to hear Steven tell me that Becca had taken a fall at a friend's house and the friend's mother thought she might need stitches near her eye. As he was starting to do a whole guilt number on me, I interrupted him. "Save the guilt for later, Steven, and just listen to two words: 'Plastic surgeon.'" He hung up, grumpy, but he did go right home and get her to the doctor.

Still, household and family fell mainly under my domain. Rosie, a Scottish woman who had taken care of the children in

Greece, eventually came to live with us here and made life livable. But, as wife, it was still my responsibility to see to it that the children were in good shape physically and mentally, the house was reasonably well kept, food was in the refrigerator, and bills were paid. Steve, more and more, offered to help. I kept saying that helping wasn't the point — doing what I asked, it was doing it without my asking, taking responsibility, that's what I claimed to be after. In truth, though, I think I was always reluctant to give up the household reins. *Power* might be too strong a word, but maybe not. I wanted the house done the way I wanted it done. I wanted fresh flowers in the vases, even if it meant staying up until two in the morning to arrange them. I wanted good meals on the table and I enjoyed cooking them. I wanted big holiday celebrations and I was determined, no matter how hard I was working, to provide them. It was part of my definition of myself, my role as wife, a role I had no intention of abandoning. Steven didn't ask those things of me. There are times when he would have been a lot happier if I had kept it simpler. And there are times when he would have been a lot happier if I had paid more attention to his needs and wants, not exhausted all my energies on the children and the job and the household. What about him? Once he told me that he felt like he was another item on my list of things to do. Ouch, that struck home. What kind of a wife was that?

Change is never easy, particularly such fundamental change. After all, it went from me being the good *New York Times* wife to me being a fairly visible person because of my own accomplishments. It's uncomfortable for me to be with Steven and have someone recognize me and not him, though he's a pretty familiar face to news junkies. As our roles continue to evolve, change is still hard. We're blessed, though, by how much we love each other. To be more exact, crazy nuts about each other. Someone once told me that young people were duped by Romeo and Juliet, that what they shared was rare, that most people never come close to a romance like that. Well, lucky us. We're in the rare category. *Household Magazine* in 1870 published a fable about an oak and a vine. The man, of course, is the oak, the woman the vine. And the point, obviously, is that the vine can't grow independently of the oak. It's a subversive tale, designed to subjugate women. But there's a lot of truth in it for me. I could not have had the life I have had professionally had I not taken as my first job that of wife. I would never have had the confidence to do what I do without Steven's encouragement and support. And none of it would be worth anything without him.

MOTHER / DAUGHTER

At a family party celebrating my mother's latest job, my brother stood to toast her: "Mother, campaign manager, mother, consummate hostess, mother, civil rights advocate, mother, congresswoman, grandmother, convention chairman, mother, author, great-grandmother, ambassador, mother." Sending her off to her new challenge as Ambassador to the Vatican, Tommy had it right. The dominant note, no matter what others dance onto the score, no matter what age she and her children might have reached, remains "mother."

My sister once said, "Motherhood is a function of distance, not time." She meant the immediate worries of mothering, not the fundamentals of the job itself. Barbara's observation came one night when we had just flown to New Orleans for our Aunt Sissy's funeral. We had arranged to arrive at approximately the same time and then planned to rent a car for the drive to the Gulf Coast of Mississippi, where my aunt had lived. As Barbara started down the escalator to the rent-a-car desk, she heard herself paged. It was my mother, already ensconced at my aunt's, suggesting we ride a shuttle bus instead of driving; she was worried about us traveling at night. Now, we were both in our forties at the time. We had each trekked all over the world and managed to survive without helpful hints from our mother. But my sister and I were both also mothers of children who had left home. We knew exactly what our mother was doing, because we did it ourselves. The children would be gone for months, doing who knows what, and we wouldn't worry a bit. The minute they were within proximity we started fretting. Motherhood is forever.

With any luck, mothers adapt, come to understand that their children are no longer children, and treat them accordingly, although we all know cases where that's not true. And in many families eventually the roles reverse, the daughter becomes the one in charge of the mother if she lives long enough. Daughters and daughters-in-law remain the chief caretakers of the elderly in America. Still, even as our lives change, even as our children grow up and go away, that basic mothering instinct, that thing at the core of our very being that impels us to shield them against the world, remains at the ready. I remember when my son, Lee, was first brought to me after he was born. I can still feel that tiny creature in my young arms, how helpless he was. Almost as physically as I felt the surge of breastmilk coming in, I felt a surge of protectiveness seeping through me. My sister recognized that primitive response when my mother resigned from Congress hoping to be able to devote herself full-time to Barbara's care when she was dying.

That was typical. Mamma could always be counted on to come through. Intellectually, I know that she was actually away a lot of the time when we were growing up. She was off campaigning for Daddy, or accompanying him on some official trip. She always worked, for him, for the party, for the community. Even so, as I resurrect those childhood pictures in my memory, they all include Mamma. To me, she was the most beautiful woman on earth, and she seemed a constant presence. When I was little I used to fake being sick so I could stay home and play with her. She knew what I was doing, but never let on. Now I realize how many cancellations and rearrangements must have followed in the wake of my announcements that I didn't feel quite up to going to school that day. Some of the time, she'd check in on me and go about her work, leaving me with Emma Cyprian, the housekeeper, who was a much sterner taskmaster. On the rare occasions when I really was sick, Mamma would do something special, like make doll clothes with me, or whip up a bowl of my favorite dessert, floating island, a custard with islands of meringue floating on top. I'm a much more diligent cook than my mother ever was, but to this day I won't make something as time-consuming as floating island.

Barbara, who had appointed herself my teacher, became completely exasperated with me when I was about six years old because she couldn't get across the concept of how to tell time. I remember Mamma making a clock out of a paper plate with construction paper hands. We sat at the edge of her bed, going over it again and again. I never caught on. Finally, she just burst out laughing, and it was all okay. I'm sure I remember the episode so well because I was convinced I was a dumbbell, a view my sister was always ready to endorse, until Mamma's laugh just made it all seem silly. That's what she's always done, instill confidence, usually by some action — a hug, a call, a laugh, rather than words. (I'm still not great at telling time, so I was grateful when digital clocks came on the scene.) When I was older and various activities kept me at school long after buses and car pools had departed, it was always my mother who would uncomplainingly fetch me and my friends, and take them all home or back to our house for the night, thereby silently endorsing our endeavors. It was our house where people and parties were welcome.

When I was in college, my sister organized a major conference aimed at establishing a domestic Peace Corps. My mother offered to house students who needed rooms. A guy I had met the summer before reserved a space chez Boggs. He and I had dated a few times and I had liked him, but then he didn't call again, so I was curious to see what would happen. He had a terrible cough, and in the middle of the night my mother wafted into his room in her negligee and served him a hot toddy. His name was Steve Roberts and he was hooked. He always teases me that he fell in love with my mother first.

Mamma always seemed able to do six things at once, so we and everyone else asked her to do everything. She had such incredible patience. She made all the curtains in the house, most of them complicated silk draperies with linings. Keep in mind, this was a woman who worked. For the den, she chose a chintz hunting scene, and carefully cut and sewed it so that the hands, horses' heads, dogs' tails, and whips connected exactly from one panel to the next when the curtains were closed. Not only would I never have the skill to do that, I would have killed myself or someone else as I became completely exasperated in the effort. When we saw the demands she placed on herself, there was no need for her to tell us that we were expected to live up to certain standards as well. And we never wanted to disappoint her.

We wore uniforms to school, but she made many of the rest of my sister's and my clothes, including our evening dresses when we were in high school. Sometimes she'd still be stitching us into our dresses, not having time to install a zipper, while our dates were downstairs getting grilled by Daddy. Years later, when we were no longer embarrassed, we teased her that she had devised a wicked way to ensure our purity.

The most vivid scene of my mother's multidexterity impressed itself forever on me the summer I was getting married. Barbara's husband was in South America, so she came home for a few weeks with her two babies. David, who was about six months old, would not allow you to put him down. He moved from hip to hip, causing my grandmother to dub him "King David." Daddy's big vegetable garden (now tended by Steven) was in full abundance, demanding attention. And Mamma was doing all the cooking for the fifteen hundred guests invited to the wedding. I'm not making this up. Maybe I should repeat that. Mamma was doing all the cooking for fifteen hundred people. I walked into the kitchen after work one day and noticed the signs on the ovens, "Take me out at seven, Take me out at eight." There at the stove stood my mother, a baby on her hip, a spoon in her hand, and the phone crooked into her neck. In one large, swaying motion she soothed the baby, stirred the pot full of pickles, and dictated a speech into the telephone.

As one of a series of "first woman to . . . ," as in the first woman to be elected to Congress from Louisiana, in 1976 she was chosen as the first woman to preside over a national political convention. There she was, up on the podium, Madison Square Garden jammed with people, TV cameras shooting from every angle, and she hears down below her, "Hey, Maw-Maw." It was an escaped grandchild, whom she quickly scooped up and brought to the podium with her until his wayward parent showed up to claim him. Her priorities never wavered.

A hard act to follow? No kidding. But

Mamma never made me feel that way. Instead, unlike for so many other women my age, she's been a continual source of support and encouragement. When most of my friends felt their mothers slathered on the guilt, my mother was busy erasing mine. One night when my kids were probably still in elementary school, or maybe in junior high, a congressional vote forced me to stay at work late to report it. I found my mother and moaned, "Here it is nine o'clock and I'm still here, I'm worried about my kids." Mamma looked at me intently and insisted, "Cokie, those kids are fine. In fact they're great. Relax." Of course she was right. Think what a relief it was for me essentially to get permission for what I was doing from my mother. Think how unusual it was that I could simply go downstairs in the Capitol to consult her. I missed her terribly when she retired and miss her even more now that she's taken a new job far from home.

So much of the mother-daughter tension has to do with an inability to consult, or an unwillingness of either mothers or daughters to admit the value of what the other has to say, I'm convinced of that. Library stacks bulge with books by experts on this subject, I know, but I've done my share of listening over the decades. When mothers who never worked outside the home hear how much their daughters value careers, they take it as a rejection. They are hurt, and often they are jealous as well, feeling they could have "amounted to something" if they had not devoted themselves to their children. But the daughters don't even seem to give them credit for what they did do — raise a family. Rather than ask their mothers, they choose instead to rely on Berry Brazelton or Penelope Leach. Instead of days at Grandma's for the kids, it's days at Gymboree or soccer or ballet or jujitsu. So, mothers uncomfortable with this landscape, and feeling left out of it, criticize their daughters and drive them crazy. And daughters, unsure of themselves and threatened by the criticism, dismiss their mothers and make them sad.

That's not the way it's supposed to work. Mothers and daughters traditionally enjoyed the closest of ties. In the nineteenth century, writes women's historian Carroll Smith-Rosenberg, "expressions of hostility today considered routine on the part of both mothers and daughters seem to have been uncommon indeed." In what was essentially an apprenticeship system, mothers trained their daughters in domesticity. In earlier times, girls worked alongside their mothers in the fields and in the farmhouse. Mom and pop shopkeepers often kept the kids behind the counter or waiting tables with them. Girls expected to grow up to be like their mothers, and depended on their mothers', and other female relatives', assistance in the process.

Maybe we're on our way back around to that. My daughter and daughter-in-law and their friends genuinely like their mothers, I'm happy to say. And we like them enormously. These young women don't seem as single-mindedly career-driven as the women between us in age, and they expect, maybe unrealistically, to both work and raise families with some kind of balance. They have the same great advantage that I did of watching a mother juggle. That allows them, if they choose, to more easily repeat our lives rather than reject them. They have the additional advantage of a somewhat more family-friendly workplace. Not friendly enough, but a lot friendlier than it was when my cohorts broke into those buildings. We're not any different from guys, we kept proclaiming, so hire us and promote us. We couldn't then say, well, actually we are different and we need maternity leave and benefit packages with child care. That took the next crowd coming in after us.

Daughters of women my age have something else going for them, they have grandmothers. Many of the women a few years younger than I am waited so long to have children, their parents were already elderly by the time the next generation of babies arrived. In contrast, my mother's first grandchild came when she was forty-four, my mother-in-law's at forty-nine. My daughter loved spending time with these still energetic grandmothers, listening to their different life experiences, extracting the common threads of womanhood. Over sheets of cookie dough or stacks of campaign data, Becca absorbed the wisdom of older women and observed that intelligence does not depend on job descriptions.

My grandmothers were so important to me, I felt so lucky to have them. I'm delighted my daughter feels the same way about hers. Coco, my mother's mother, sported spike-heeled shoes and bright red hair. Grandee stuck to the sensible brogans and soft white waves. Their lives seemed entirely removed from each other's, but they weren't really. They enjoyed each other's company, in that way that women pulled together over the years often do. The same's true of my mother and mother-in-law. Even though they don't see each other that often, there's something between them when they do. It was especially true at Lee's wedding, when Steve's father had just died. My mother literally locked arms with my mother-in-law, so the two of them became a team.

A Mother's Day poll taken recently reveals that American women are closer to their mothers than some of the modern literature would imply. Nearly all talk to their mothers at least once a week (the poll doesn't tell us whether those conversations are pleasant or not), nearly half speak almost every day, and a great many do solicit their mothers' advice on child rearing. My mother moved to Europe at the end of last year, so it's hard to talk to her more than once a week these days; my daughter and I, on the other hand, talk all the time. I call her, she calls me. We talk about everything from radio to recipes. In watching the women in the family, she seems to have taken ingredients from each for her own still stewing gumbo.

She loves the political world of my mother, and for a few years worked producing radio and TV commercials for candidates. She loves the intellectual and brain-teasing world of Steve's mother, so she joins book clubs and pores over crossword puzzles. She loves my world of journalism, she's hosted her own cable TV show, and now produces and reports for radio. Becca eased into the reporting part of her job and I gently teased her about it not too long ago, asking her if she had noticed that she's now — *ahem* — a public radio reporter? She replied, "I know, I know, and the truth is, I love it." And is really good at it, her proud mother might add. She loves the domestic world of all of us, and creates wonderful concoctions in the kitchen. She comes home from her demanding duties for the holidays to make the big family celebrations possible. She decorates, shops, wraps, and cooks and keeps me laughing all the while. She gives her new mother-in-law some giggles as well, in a relationship that's sure to blossom over the years. She's one of the most competent, smart, funny people I've ever met.

Even when she was a little girl she was willing to exert herself. I remember when she was five she came home from school complaining about the "boring" spelling words, *at, cat, bat.* She had learned them on *Sesame Street* when she was two. I asked if she wanted me to talk to her teacher about it. "No, I'll do it," my five-year-old responded. Her teacher said she could choose her own words from her reading. That night I asked what she had chosen. "Psychiatrist," she answered. Now you know that teacher still thinks I put her up to that. Becca's always been a total delight, so what's she doing in San Francisco?

Of course, I know exactly what she's doing there. She's becoming her own person, not that she isn't already, and establishing her marriage away from the expectations of extended family. I did exactly the same thing, and I completely approve of it, at least with my head. My heart misses her, and her brother who moved to London, more all the time. It's a funny reaction for someone as busy as I am whose nest has been empty for ten years now. But it's because, no matter what else I've ever done, for almost thirty years, my first definition of self has been "mother."

From the moment I watched the first baby emerge from my body, to the moment I watched the second walk down the aisle to form a new family, my first responsibility was to those two people. When they're little people, you can actually feel that responsibility in your weary bones, there's no such thing as calling in sick on mommyhood. How do they survive? Lee was a pretty cautious kid, but Becca was death-defying. At thirteen months, she managed to put a rent-a-car into gear and drove out of a drive-in laundry in California. I went tearing out to save her by driving the car into another one. You can imagine the accident report: age of driver, one year. That was just the beginning with her. But as every mother knows, the fear of physical danger is nothing compared to the worry about emotional upset. When they were in school, a bell rang in my head every day at three o'clock — the kids were home, what was happening? I'd call and get the usual responses. Conversation with son: "How are you?" "Fine." "What did you do today?" "Not much." Conversation with daughter: "How are you?" "Great." (Or terrible, or some superlative.) "What did you do today?" "Well, in first period we did. . . ." Half an hour later I was still holding the phone at my ear. Lee would occasionally bare his soul, but only when I was away. He'd see my phone number, call me at one or two in the morning, and pour out his problems. Then he'd go happily to sleep leaving me wide awake in some motel room in Iowa, my arms aching I wanted so much to hold him. He told me later that he would have never talked to me so frankly had I been home sleeping in my own bed.

With a daughter it was different. I'm not saying that Becca told me her inmost thoughts, but we did talk a lot. We were also buddies — in the kitchen, in the shopping malls, on the phone. It was tough for me when she left for college because it not only meant both of my children were now gone from home, it also meant losing one of my best friends. I don't know what I would have done if I didn't have a busy work life to occupy me. The kids were awfully generous about coming home, and bringing their friends around. Lee moved back in for a few months after college when he was between apartments and I found out that all of this talk about boomerang kids misses an essential point. They are able to come home because we like them, and they like us. The famous generation gap's now nothing more than a crack.

Even after Lee moved out he still came home for Sunday night dinners. After a while he started bringing Liza McDonald with him. He had first met her years before when they were teenage pages at the Capitol. Now she was back here as a reporter, of all things. Briefly, Liza worked with me at ABC, where she became my friend too. As I got to know her well, I knew this was a young woman any mother would die for, and I was scared to death Lee might blow it. As I sensitively once told Becca, "I have a higher vested interest in a daughter-in-law than a son-in-law. She'll be in the kitchen with me, while he'll be in the den watching football with Daddy." It wasn't a terribly modern view of marriage, but a pretty realistic one. Fortunately, Lee proved again that he's no dummy, and now we have a dear new daughter in Liza. Though I teased about the son-in-law, it is of course no joke — this guy will be your baby girl's husband. Fortunately, Becca's guy, Dan Hartman, is a great one, so we're lucky indeed.

As a mother, watching your children go off to start their own families is both heartening and hard. Now it's someone else who occupies first place in their lives, someone else they will call to say they've arrived safely. And they have suddenly become part of a whole new family tree; we are but one of their extended branches. Maybe consciously, maybe not, both our kids married people whose parents have been married for more than thirty years. These are families in which people love each other and love our children. We will have a wonderful time being grandparents together. All of us mothers are being good, so far, but of course we want to be grandmothers. And we want our daughters to be mothers because there's no other role as demanding, as terrifying, as maddening, and as rewarding as that of mother.

I always wanted children, but not until

they were actually part of my life did I realize that I could love that fiercely, or get that angry. Even when the kids were very little, I always found them fascinating people. Every parent says this because it's true; it's remarkable how formed those personalities are from the minute they pop. Mothers and mothers-in-law can tell you some home truths about yourself and your spouse as you embark on bringing up those boisterous babies. Grandmothers can tell you some truths about your mother as well.

ENTERPRISER

When I was at Wellesley, I used to study at the Harvard Business School library. It was right across the river from Steve's dorm, so at the end of a day at the books, I could wander over and hope to "run into" him. I don't know why they let Wellesley women into the library in those years. They didn't allow women into the Business School itself until 1962. That's right. Even so, somehow as a sex we managed; women have thrived in business, particularly as business owners, calling somewhat into question that hallowed Harvard degree.

The most recent Census Bureau numbers tell us that women own one-third of all U.S. businesses, a total of about eight million enterprises. They employ about a quarter of the work force, roughly the same as the *Fortune* 500 combined, and generate more than two and a quarter trillion dollars in sales. The growth of women-owned businesses outpaces that of all businesses by nearly two to one. And once a woman starts a business, she's more likely to keep it going than her male counterpart.

We know that women have been in business at least since the "good wife" of Proverbs who "considers a field and buys it" and "perceives that her merchandise is profitable." In this country women were licensed as tavern owners in Massachusetts as early as the 1600s, and women regularly ran businesses while their husbands were away at sea, or at war, or when they were widowed. In a wonderful book called *Daughters of America; or, Women of the Century*, written in 1883, the author, Phebe Hanaford, quotes from a contemporary New York newspaper: "Some curious facts relative to various businesses carried on in New York City by women are made known in the latest directory published at the metropolis. The proportion of men to women in business where the women stand as their own representatives is 4,479 women to 37,203 men." More than 10 percent! The paper goes on to cite the businesses — billiard and lager-beer saloon owners, blacksmith, druggist, pawnbroker, wood-engraver, doctor.

Most of these early American entrepreneurs and other enterprising women have been lost in the mists of history. But a few survived the anonymity of women in the annals, and some of their tales are worth telling or retelling. One is Margaret Brent, called "Gentleman Margaret Brent" because the men of seventeenth-century Maryland didn't know how else to address her. When she arrived in the colony in 1638, she was already acting as a lawyer. (How that happened the histories don't tell us.) Then, thanks to the intervention of her cousin, Lord Baltimore, she and her sister took possession of a sizable tract of land, and thanks to the indebtedness of her brother, she acquired his very substantial property as well. (Had she been married, she would not have been able to own anything, a common-law role that did not change until the late nineteenth century in most parts of the country.) Margaret Brent continued to amass land, and therefore power, and soon became legal counsel to the governor. Can you imagine the judges and opposing lawyers? What were they supposed to do with this woman? They had no choice but to pay attention to her, which turned out to be a good thing for Maryland.

The civil war in England meant a summons to Governor Calvert to return. While he was there, two Virginians, one of them, by the way, my direct ancestor William Claiborne, took control of Maryland. They were Protestants, Maryland was Catholic. Calvert came back, raised an army to retake the colony, and then died, first naming Margaret Brent as executor of his estate. The soldiers Calvert had hired had not been paid, or even fed, and an uprising was on the horizon. Miss Brent first held them at bay by importing corn from Virginia and slaughtering some of her own cattle to feed them. Then, when the Calvert estate turned out not to be sufficient to compensate the soldiers, she used her power of attorney for the new governor to draw on the colony's proprietor, Lord Baltimore's, estate. She sold enough cattle to pay the mutinous army, and the soldiers went away peacefully. When from his perch in England Lord Baltimore strenuously objected to the Maryland Assembly, he was disappointed in the response. Instead of rebuking Brent, the assemblymen commended her, saying, "It was better for the Colony's safety at that time in her hands than in any man's else in the whole Province." The assembly was ready to praise her, but not to give her a vote, which she demanded as a freeholder. In fact, she asked for two votes, one for herself and one for her client, Governor Green. It was one of the few fights she lost. Before retiring to Virginia at the age of fifty-six, she was involved in one hundred and twenty-four court cases, including many jury trials, and won them all.

Among the enterprising women in American history, one of my personal favorites is Elizabeth Ann Seton, probably because I have such respect for the nuns who taught me. She's actually Saint Elizabeth, officially canonized by the Catholic Church in 1974, the first native-born American to achieve sainthood. I bet a lot of the people who dealt with her didn't consider her a saint. She accomplished so much, she had to step on a few toes along the way. Mother Seton's biographies always include a line that I just love, it goes something like "she is credited with founding the American parochial school system." That's one of those statements where my reaction is, "Excuse me? Could I hear a little more please? That's totally extraordinary." And, of course, her story is. She went from riches to rags — born in New York shortly before the Revolution, her father was a noted doctor and she was a well educated young woman, someone raised to show concern for the poor. She married a wealthy New York merchant, William Seton, and proceeded to have five children before he lost first his fortune, then his health. On what was supposed to be a restorative trip to Italy in 1803, Seton died, and the Anglican Elizabeth was consoled by Italian Catholic friends. After Elizabeth returned to New York she converted to Catholicism, much to the horror of her family. The family cut her off, leaving her and the five children destitute.

A Catholic priest in Baltimore asked her to move there to start a school for girls, which she did with the help of several other women. It was either the first or one of the first Catholic elementary schools in the United States, depending on which history you read. She did establish the first Catholic child care institution, the Orphan Asylum of Philadelphia, in 1814. That same year, five children not withstanding, Seton founded a religious order, the Daughters (now Sisters) of Charity, the first one to originate in this country. By the time she died, in 1821, the order had spread out to twenty communities across the nation, starting schools and opening orphanages. Think of what it must have been like for those women, setting out on their own in early America, battling anti-Catholicism in order to educate children and take care of the poor and sick. Nothing easy about any of it.

Clara Barton is another one whose story intrigues me. There's an old amusement park not far from my house where we used to hang out as teenagers. All that's left is an antique carousel and a children's theater, where Steve and I took our kids when they were small. Next door is Clara Barton House, run by the National Park Service. I always meant to learn more about this neighbor of mine. Finally, when the local Red Cross chapter asked me to present some awards to its star volunteers, I did. One of those intrepid Massachusetts women, Clara Barton established a free school in New Jersey which grew from six to six hundred students in one year. When the school hired a male principal, she quit and moved to Washington where she worked in the Patent Office. With the arrival of a new administration, she lost her patronage and her job. Without work, Barton became "sickly," a pattern that repeated itself throughout her life. She went back to work in 1860, but then the Civil War broke out, allowing her to follow what was clearly her calling as the "Angel of the Battlefield."

The night before the horrific battle of Antietam she wrote, "I was faint but could not eat; weary, but could not sleep; depressed, but could not weep." Her fears were more than justified — twenty-three thousand soldiers lay dead or wounded the next day. Clara Barton constantly drove mule wagons through fire, crossed battle lines, and, most remarkably, cut red tape to nurse sick soldiers and distribute supplies to them. She badgered President Lincoln into setting up a bureau of records to identify the missing and the dead. In the summer of 1865 at Andersonville she oversaw the marking of thirteen thousand graves with headboards. As someone whose father disappeared in an airplane that was never found, I have always had tremendous empathy for families of the missing in action. Clara Barton was the first to recognize the need for some certainty about death.

With war's end, she became "sickly" again (clearly depressed due to inaction) and headed for Europe to rest. That was a joke; she soon learned about the International Red Cross and was back in battle, this time in the Franco-Prussian War, where she made her way to the front. The Red Cross became her life. On her return to the United States, she established the American chapter. There's another one of those historical statements that boggles the mind. Congress in the late 1800s feared nothing more than "foreign entanglements." So it took tireless lobbying to finally convince the Senate to ratify the Geneva Convention, forming the American Red Cross, in 1882. Even more remarkable, Barton got the whole organization to go along with what was called the "American amendment," which she authored. It mandated the Red Cross to provide relief for victims of natural disasters as well as war, an exponential increase in its duties. What politics must have been involved in that little coup! And what a life it then meant for Barton, who was off to the Ohio floods in 1884, providing relief to victims of Russian and Armenian famines, then at the age of seventy-seven, to Cuba for the Spanish-American War, where she was back on the battlefield. She set a pattern for all future wars, where Red Cross nurses have brought care and comfort by the tens of thousands. Barton herself was not much of an organization woman, and she was forced to step down as president of the Red Cross in 1904. But she continued her relief work until she died at the age of ninety-one.

Madam C. J. Walker suffered from no lack of organizational skills. I first learned about this fellow Louisianian from my ABC friend and colleague A'Lelia Bundles, Ms. Walker's great-great-granddaughter, who's now writing a book about her exceptional ancestor. In 1867, Sarah Breedlove was the first member of her family born to freedom. But her family's release from slavery did not mean release from the no-exit life of poverty of a

Louisiana sharecropper. Orphaned at age seven, married at fourteen, soon a mother, and widowed at twenty, she supported herself and her daughter, A'Lelia, with backbreaking work as a washerwoman for almost twenty years, first in Vicksburg, then in St. Louis. She managed miraculously to send her daughter to school, and joined the missionary society at church, where she met for the first time black people with education, culture, and money. The St. Louis World's Fair in 1904 introduced the young woman not only to prominent black leaders, but also to beautiful black women. Women with hair. Like many poor people with bad diets, Sarah Breedlove McWilliams had lost much of her hair, in an era when the Gibson Girl, with her upswept mane, was the standard of beauty. McWilliams's determination to grow her hair turned her into the first American black woman millionaire.

She claimed that the formula for her hair products came to her in a dream. It might have come to her by trial and error in a pharmacy where she worked after moving to Denver to be with her brother's widow and children. Wherever the formula came from, it worked. Her own luxurious head of hair attested to that fact better than any advertisement. After marrying journalist C. J.

Walker, she christened the product Madam C. J. Walker's Wonderful Hair Grower and sold it door to door. Along with Walker's help in publicizing it, and her own talent for self-promotion, the Walker System, as she called it, became a huge success. Madam Walker started her own cosmetics company, hiring thousands of women to sell her products, as she became famous the world over. She eventually moved the headquarters to Indianapolis, but she set up house in Harlem. Her daughter A'Lelia later ran the mansion, known as "The Dark Tower," as a salon for black artists and intellectuals.

The flamboyant Madam Walker not only made vast sums of money, she also gave it away. Born a sharecropper's daughter, she died a renowned philanthropist. It's hard to wrap your mind around this kind of achievement. The hurdles she had to vault — poverty, ignorance, racism, sexism — made her a great believer in self-help. But Walker believed in helping others as well, contributing to the NAACP, plus dozens of black charities, and providing girls with scholarships to Tuskegee Institute. She promoted female talent and spurred on the sales of the some three thousand women who worked for her with prizes and bonuses. The charter of her business specified that only a woman could serve as president. And when she died at age fifty-one, her daughter took over the cosmetics empire.

Hiring and promoting women also characterized Margaret Rudkin's approach to a successful business. I love this story because it's rooted in such practicality. A doctor in 1937 told Mrs. Rudkin that he thought her son's asthma might stem from an allergy to chemical additives in commercially baked bread. So, like a good mother, she started baking her own. But first she did a little homework, as all good girls do, studying nutrition and holistic medicine. She came up with a whole-wheat bread made with all fresh ingredients, and her son seemed to get better. At least he improved enough that the doctor ordered the bread for himself and other patients. Thus was born a little enterprise called Pepperidge Farm.

First Rudkin sold her breads to doctors through the mail. Soon she had to hire a neighbor to help her bake, and expand the kitchen into the garage and stable. It wasn't long before she was peddling her products wholesale. And peddle she did. She'd walk into a store with bread, butter, and knife, give a taste to the owner, and hook him. Two years after she started the business, Pepperidge Farm was selling twenty-five thousand loaves of bread a week. Expansion was impossible during World War II, but once the war was over a new plant started turning out four thousand loaves of bread an hour. Yet Rudkin still insisted the dough be hand kneaded and the ingredients fresh. She hired women because she simply thought they were better at baking bread than men. Hard work was expected, and above average pay provided.

Like Madam Walker, Maggie Rudkin promoted herself to a fare-thee-well and she had the advantage of a new invention called television. But it was a *Reader's Digest* article that put her on the international map. Despite constant growth in the business, she insisted the quality stay high and the bread fresh. A two-day shelf life was the maximum she allowed, but then Rudkin did something ingenious with the stale leftovers — she made stuffing, and sold it at a profit. Next it was cookies, created from a Belgian recipe after she and her husband went around Europe with the tough task of tasting cookies wherever they went. When I was a new bride I always served Pepperidge Farm Pirouettes with my desserts; I thought they were quite elegant and sophisticated-looking. By the time Maggie Rudkin sold the bakery she had started as a response to her little boy's asthma, it was a company with thirty-two million dollars in annual sales. Campbell Soup bought it in 1960 for twenty-eight million dollars in Campbell's stock. Though she was clearly an astute businesswoman, Rudkin understood the tenor of the times. She marketed herself as the ultimate housewife, and her multimillion-dollar business as a homey little bakery where no one had to feel threatened by a woman in charge.

In just a few years, women are expected to own half the businesses in this country. What's not clear is whether that will affect all women — whether that will make a difference in this ongoing argument about a woman's place.

A WOMAN'S PLACE

"A woman's place is in the House . . . and in the Senate," the T-shirts and buttons proclaim at women's political events. "A Woman's Place Is in Uniform," trumpets a book about women in the military. "A woman's place is at the typewriter," declared *Fortune* magazine back in 1935. That was convenient for the economy and so it was decreed. A few years later a woman's place was in the factory or in the nursing corps because that was essential for the war effort. Then a woman's place was in the home. And now? A woman's place is anywhere she wants it to be. Fine, but who's taking care of the children? That's the question that keeps us roiled up over this issue.

Recently the country got all in a snit over the case of a baby apparently killed by his baby-sitter in Boston. Were people demanding the head of the baby-sitter? No, quite the contrary, it was the mother who came in for abuse by the radio callers and the editorial writers. She went to work three days a week, coming home at lunchtime to breast-feed, even though her husband had a perfectly good job. What kind of mother was she? Obviously, a selfish, greedy one who was willing to leave her children in the care of an inexperienced young woman. Wait a minute. Suppose she had gone out at night with her husband and left the babies with a teenager? What then? And didn't society just direct thousands of mothers to leave their children in another's care by requiring that welfare mothers go to work? Could we make up our minds here, please?

No, probably not, because we're still confused about this issue of a woman's place. We're confused because we know that no matter what else a woman is doing, she's also caretaking and we worry that a woman "out at work" might leave someone, especially her children, without care. That's what's at the heart of this sometimes vicious debate. Sure, a lot of other, much less noble, attitudes also underlie these arguments. Plenty of people still think that women are just plain uppity and they see a woman's place as someplace to put her. But I think it's the question of the children, and now old people as well, that truly troubles us. And women with children often find whatever choice they make uncomfortable.

That wasn't always true. For most of human history men and women worked together in the same place and each one's work complemented the other's. No one thought the farmer's job was more important than the farm wife's. Neither could manage without the other. Teenage relatives often moved in to help care for the children, to protect them from household hazards like open fires while the busy mother made the soap and the candles, spun the cloth, pieced together the clothes, fixed the food. Women gathered together to help with large chores, and visited as they worked. They also congregated to attend to births and deaths, taking comfort from each other's company.

Whenever I think of the courage it took to leave everything and everyone behind to come to this continent in the early years of colonization, I am struck by the fortitude of those settlers. First the trip across the ocean, then in later generations the trek across the continent, required women to "do it all." The history of the movement west is one of extraordinary men and women overcoming incredible odds together. It was the industrial revolution that changed everything. Men went out to work for wages, and they were paid for the hours they put in, not the tasks they completed. (Poor women went into the factories, or to domestic work, as well. In 1850 women comprised 13 percent of the paid labor force; this question of women's work is one directly related to economic class.) Suddenly, what women did at home lost its value because there was no paycheck attached. Repetitive housework replaced home manufacture as women's crafts moved into assembly-line production. And that's what we've been struggling with ever since. Doing work that is economically rewarded and socially recognized means leaving home. That could change with the information revolution, as machines make it possible to work just about anywhere. But I think it's unlikely to alter the fact that women aren't paid for their jobs as nurturers, and it still leaves women at home isolated from other women.

It's important, I think, for young women today to understand that they are not the first generation to deal with these questions. That's part of the reason I've tried in this little book to give some sense of the scope of women's work over many generations, to give today's women a glimpse of women who have gone before them. But knowing that you're not the first to have to cope with a problem doesn't necessarily make solving it any easier. And for reasons that I don't fully understand, women make each other's lives harder by trying to impose their own choices on their sisters. Again, it's important to be clear eyed here that we are talking only about women privileged enough to have choices. If society makes some statement about mothers and children, it should relate to all mothers and children.

Over the last forty years, I've watched this argument go full circle. When I was in high school and college, my friends' mothers did not work, and there was definitely a stigma attached to female employment. My own mother escaped it because she worked for and with my father, which was acceptable. Keep in mind, this was not long after World War II, when there was an organized effort to get women out of the workplace. A women's magazine article in 1951 (the year I was in third grade) lists the pros and cons of the author's decision to quit her office job. Among the items she counts as "lost" along with "the sense of personal achievement" and "praise for a good piece of work," is "One baseless vanity. I realize now (and still blush over it) that during my working days I felt that my ability to earn was an additional flower in my wreath of accomplishments." On the "found" list along with "normalcy" and "intimacy" is "Improved Appearance. Shinier hair, nicer hands, better manicures, are the products of those chance twenty-minute periods that turn up in the busiest days of women who don't go to business." That would have convinced me.

With the advent of modern feminism, it was women at home who were looked down upon by their fellow females. What were they doing with their educations? How could they allow themselves to be so dependent on a male? Didn't they know he could up and leave them penniless at any moment? The women's movement gave lip service to the concept of choice, but didn't mean it. The strong message: Women, to have any worth, you must go to work, show that you are just like a man.

Now, there's a swing back to stigmatizing the at-work woman if she is a mother. Some of these critiques are ridiculous. I remember reading one in our local newspaper where the author opined that a working mother wouldn't be able to bake with the children, hand down the cookie recipes from generation to generation. I thought of my cabinet full of cookie cutters — Christmas cookie cutters, Hanukkah cookie cutters, Valentine cookie cutters, Halloween cookie cutters — and the hours I have put in rolling the dough, overseeing the decoration ("No, you can't dump a whole bottle of sprinkles on one cookie") and all I could do was laugh. Then I got angry. Who was she to question my choices? And why did she want to? To validate her own.

Obviously, there's good reason to be concerned about children and if this country's ready to have a serious conversation about children, I'm all for it. But that conversation goes to far more fundamental questions than how some middle- and upper-middle-class women spend a few years of their lives. Let's talk about children in danger from their parents and their neighborhoods, children who are hungry, children who can't get educated in the public schools, children whose parents use them as pawns in domestic wars, children who are lonely, children who have no hope for their futures, if we truly want to concern ourselves with America's kids. Children who have two parents married to each other and who care enough about them to worry about work versus home are already well ahead of the game. I don't mean to belittle the difficulty in making those choices, I'm just trying to put them in perspective.

Women would do well to take the long view in making personal decisions, as we always have. The number of years we have children at home, particularly preschool children, is few. The number of years available to move ahead in the work force is many, assuming we live full lifespans. Putting career on the back, or at least the middle, burner in the years children are small makes a lot of sense to me. That doesn't necessarily mean staying home full-time. For me, that would have been a disaster. I need to work for my spiritual and emotional well-being, and while that might not be admirable, it's true. In interim periods between jobs I've suffered genuine depression, and believe me, that's not good for the children. I was a better mother because I worked.

But there were times along the way when I turned down good jobs because they weren't appropriate for my family. As we were leaving Los Angeles, some feelers came my way about anchoring a new TV newscast. I didn't even pursue them because we were moving to Greece. While I was in Greece, the CBS foreign editor talked to me about being the network's "woman in Europe." It sounded very glamorous, but I would have been traveling all the time. Steven's job required nonstop travel, so it didn't seem at all fair to the kids for both of us to be gone constantly. I said no.

That's not to say that there have never been times my family's suffered because of my job. Of course there were. The kids still resent the long wait for dinner every night, the calls saying that we'd be home, and then the calls saying we'd be later than expected. I'm sure there were times that it would have been more comfortable and comforting for them if I had been home after school, times that it would have been helpful to them if I were available to drive them on errands or to see friends. As your kids get older they don't want you around most of the time, but when they want you, they want you. Unfortunately, there's no way to schedule those times, they just happen. You can schedule the things you know about, and there Steven and I had a pretty good track record. We were there for everything important — the adjustments to new schools, the activities, the performances, and I was very involved in the PTAs over the years. As we look back on it, there's only one big event Steven and I missed, at least only one that we know about — Becca's first dance.

It was the weekend before the 1984 election, I was in Los Angeles, Steve was in Chicago. We each called home to discover that Becca had gone to the homecoming dance. She was a freshman, her date a senior. Lee was decidedly unforthcoming with the details. He didn't know who was driving, when the invitation was issued, what time she would be home. "What was she wearing?" I asked. "Something blue and shiny of yours," he replied. I felt guilty and angry that I wasn't there, cheated out of my daughter's first dance, worried that no rules had been set with the boy. Of course, there was an adult staying with the kids, but that's not the same as a parent when it comes to your first big date. Steve and I each kept calling to check on her. It got later and later, still no Becca. We called each other in a panic and stayed on the phone so long that we realized she couldn't get through to us if she did show up. When she finally checked in she explained that she was the last kid in the car to be delivered home because her parents were away and it wouldn't matter. Oh great. Luckily, she was a good kid, as was her brother.

So yes, there were times that my work got in the way of my family. And there were times when my family got in the way of my work. It will continue to do so. Children might be our first responsibility but let's not kid ourselves, women care for the whole family, which includes the family of friends. A few years ago the *New York Times* published a poll which revealed that two thirds of all women aged eighteen to fifty-five work outside the home, half said they provided at least half the family income, and almost 20 percent were the sole providers. Regardless of job, 90 percent said they were the principal caretakers for their families. I guess the other 10 percent just haven't figured it out yet. And this nurturing goes on forever. My thirtieth college reunion class book includes this entry: "George's parents are still in good health and maintain active lives. We think it is remarkable that his 81-year-old father and 78-year-old mother look after George's 100-year-old grandmother who still lives alone in her Wisconsin farmhouse."

When my sister was sick, work took a backseat. When Nina Totenberg's husband was sick, I spent time every day with her and him that I would otherwise have spent at work. Just recently my father-in-law died, both my kids got married, and my mother sold her apartment here and moved to Rome, which involved packing up fifty-seven years of her life in Washington. Each one of those events took precedence over my work. Becca's wedding came close to being a full-time job, but since both she and I had those already, it couldn't be. One day, an editor at National Public Radio was flabbergasted when three of his reporters told him that if he wanted to reach us, we'd be in my kitchen. Steve's garden was in bounteous bloom and we had declared "canning day," where we bottled and pickled and froze all the produce, trading recipes and stories as we went along. My aunt Sissy used to say that housework wasn't hard, it was just lonely. Not if you bring in your buddies to share it with you.

Just a few weeks before she died at the age of ninety-seven, former senator Margaret Chase Smith wrote an introduction to the book *Outstanding Women Members of Congress*. " 'Where is the proper place of women?' is a question I have often been asked," she begins. "The quizzers have asked this question ambitiously, defiantly, hopefully — and just plain inquisitively. But it has been asked so many times in so many ways and by so many types of people that, of necessity, my answer has had to transcend the normal and understandable prejudice that a woman might have. My answer is short and simple — woman's proper place is everywhere. Individually it is where the particular woman is happiest and best fitted — in the home as wives and mothers; in organized civic, business and professional groups; in industry and business, both management and labor; and in government and politics. Generally, if there is any proper place for women today, it is that of alert and responsible citizens in the fullest sense of the word."

Because our communities and our country need us just as the children do, the country requires the services of women soldiers and politicians and businesswomen and club-women and consumer and civil rights activists and women helping other women get off welfare and nurses and nuns. The country needs us to be sisters and aunts and friends and mothers and daughters and wives first in the literal sense, and then in the figurative one — sisters to society, caretakers. Women can complain forever about how our devotion to those roles is not remunerated, that society doesn't compensate us for our nurturing. And frankly, I don't think we'll ever solve that problem. If we want public recognition and financial reward we will continue to have to "do it all." But that's not such a terrible thing. One piece of advice for young women: don't worry about it so much. There are times when life's emotionally and physically exhausting, and times when sleep deprivation seems likely to do you in, but you'll make it. Women are tough, we've managed to keep all the balls in the air for a very long time.

These are issues I've been puzzling about

most of my adult life. Recently, I unearthed a journal where I occasionally jotted down my thoughts while we were living in Greece. I found an entry from twenty-one years ago, when I was thirty-three years old and contemplating our family's next move. "No one writes about women like me, and we probably form a large group, who daily make the choice about our career, family, etc. It's not a one-time decision, but a continual one. And we can get so trapped by any alternative — the pure kid, pure work or balance. So can a man, of course, but in nothing like the same way." That was a long time ago, and so far I haven't gotten trapped. I've been blessed with a gloriously happy marriage, two fabulous kids now safely launched, the many joys of family and friendship, and a fine, fulfilling career. By living on this earth long enough, I've learned that clichés are clichés because they are true. It's true that you'll only have one opportunity to witness your baby's first step, to hold your dying sister's hand, to see your mother credentialed by the Pope, to hold your mother-in-law as she learns of her husband's death, to celebrate thirty years with your husband. There will always be another job.

So what is a woman's place? For most women it's many places, different places at

Suggested Reading

Baxandall, Rosalyn, and Linda Gordon. *America's Working Women: A Documentary History from 1600 to the Present.* New York: W. W. Norton & Company, 1995.

Bird, Caroline. *Enterprising Women.* New York: W. W. Norton & Company, 1976.

Chafe, William H. *The Paradox of Change: American Women in the 20th Century.* New York: Oxford University Press, 1991.

Cott, Nancy F. *The Bonds of Womanhood: "Woman's Sphere" in New England, 1780–1835, 2nd Edition.* New Haven: Yale University Press, 1997.

Cowan, Ruth Schwartz. *More Work for Mother: The Ironies of Household Technology from the Open Hearth to the Microwave.* New York: Basic Books, 1983.

Evans, Sara M. *Born for Liberty: A History of Women in America.* New York: Free Press, 1997.

Faust, Drew Gilpin. *Mothers of Invention: Women of the Slaveholding South in the American Civil War.* Chapel Hill: University of North Carolina Press, 1996.

Hanaford, Phebe A. *Daughters of America; or, Women of the Century*. Augusta, Maine: True and Company, 1883.

Hartmann, Susan M. *American Women in the 1940's: The Home Front and Beyond*. Boston: Twayne Publishing, 1982.

Heinemann, Sue. *Timelines of American Women's History*. New York: Roundtable Press Books/Perigee Books, 1996.

Hoffman, Ronald, and Peter J. Albert, editors. *Women in the Age of the American Revolution*. Charlottesville: United States Capitol Historical Society by the University Press of Virginia, 1989.

James, Edward T., editor. *Notable American Women 1607–1950: A Biographical Dictionary*, Volumes I — III. Cambridge: The Belknap Press of Harvard University Press, 1971.

Juster, Norton. *So Sweet to Labor: Rural Women in America 1865–1895*. New York: Viking Press, 1979.

Larson, C. Kay. *'Til I Come Marching Home: A Brief History of American Women in World War II*. Pasadena, Maryland: The Minerva Press, 1995.

Lerner, Gerda. *The Majority Finds Its Past: Placing Women in History*. New York: Oxford University Press, 1979.

Litoff, Judy Barrett, and David C. Smith.

We're in This War, Too: World War II Letters from American Women in Uniform. New York: Oxford University Press, 1994.

Matthews, Glenna. *Just a Housewife: The Rise and Fall of Domesticity in America.* New York: Oxford University Press, 1987.

Riley, Glenda, and Richard W. Etulain. *By Grit & Grace: Eleven Women Who Shaped the American West.* Golden, Colorado: Fulcrum Publishing, 1997.

Robertson, Nan. *The Girls in the Balcony.* New York: Fawcett Columbine, 1992.

Sherr, Lynn. *Failure Is Impossible.* New York: Times Books, 1995.

Sherr, Lynn, and Jurate Kazickas. *Susan B. Anthony Slept Here.* New York: Times Books, 1976, 1994.

Smith-Rosenberg, Carroll. *Disorderly Conduct: Visions of Gender in Victorian America.* New York: Oxford University Press, 1985.

The employees of Thorndike Press hope you have enjoyed this Large Print book. All our Large Print titles are designed for easy reading, and all our books are made to last. Other Thorndike Press Large Print books are available at your library, through selected bookstores, or directly from us.

For information about titles, please call:

(800) 257-5157
To share your comments, please write:

Publisher
Thorndike Press
P.O. Box 159
Thorndike, Maine 04986